JOSEPH ANDREWS

A Satire of Modern Times

GW00725406

Twayne's Masterwork Studies

Robert Lecker, General Editor

JOSEPH ANDREWS

A Satire of Modern Times

Simon Varey

TWAYNE PUBLISHERS • BOSTON
A Division of G.K. Hall & Co.

Joseph Andrews: A Satire of Modern Times
Simon Varey

Twayne's Masterwork Studies No. 58

Copyright 1990 by G. K. Hall & Co.
All rights reserved.
Published by Twayne Publishers
A division of G. K. Hall & Co.
70 Lincoln Street
Boston, Massachusetts 02111

Copyediting supervised by Barbara Sutton.
Book production and book design by Gabrielle B. McDonald.
Typeset in 10/14 Sabon
by Compset, Inc., Beverly, Massachusetts.

The paper used in this publication meets the minimum requirements
of American National Standard for Information Sciences—Permanence
of Paper for Printed Library Materials, ANSI Z39.48-1984. ∞™

Printed and bound in the United States of America.

Library of Congress Cataloging-in-Publication Data

Varey, Simon, 1951–
      Joseph Andrews : a satire of modern times / Simon Varey.
            p.   cm. — (Twayne's masterwork studies ; no. 58)
      Includes bibliographical references and references.
      1. Fielding, Henry, 1707–1754. History of the adventures of
Joseph Andrews.   2. Satire, English—History and criticism.
I. Title.   II. Series.
PR3454.J67V37   1990
823'.5—dc20   90-36795
                                                                      CIP

0-8057-9431-X(hc) 10   9   8   7   6   5   4   3   2   1
0-8057-8137-4(pbk) 10   9   8   7   6   5   4   3   2   1
First published 1990.

Contents

Note on the References and Acknowledgments

Three paperback editions of *Joseph Andrews* readily available in the United States print exactly the same text: the Riverside Edition (Boston: Houghton Mifflin, 1961), issued in one version with *Shamela* and in another without; the World's Classics Edition (Oxford: Oxford University Press, 1980), which also includes *Shamela;* and the Wesleyan Edition (Middletown, Conn.: Wesleyan University Press, 1984), a paperback reprint of the standard, hardcover Wesleyan edition of 1967 but without *Shamela*. Martin C. Battestin edited the definitive text for the Wesleyan Edition, which has additional notes about textual matters; he also edited the Riverside Edition for the general reader rather than the textual scholar. Because all three editions are commonly in use in American colleges and universities, I have used a form of reference that makes it easy for anyone to find what I am quoting, whichever edition he or she may have. My quotations come from the Wesleyan edition, so the exact wording is identical to the other two texts, but because the page numbers obviously differ from one edition to another, I have added book and chapter references. A typical reference such as "(175; 2, 16)" means page 175 in the Wesleyan, book 2, chapter 16 in all editions.

It is my pleasure once again to thank the generous and genial staff at the William Andrews Clark Memorial Library, UCLA.

William Hogarth, *The Stage Coach, or, The Country Inn Yard* (1747).

Chronology: Henry Fielding's Life and Works

1688	Britain's bloodless, bourgeois revolution, called "glorious" by some, takes place. The Catholic King James II is deposed (officially he "abdicates") and is replaced by his Protestant daughter Mary and her Dutch husband, William of Orange. Births of Alexander Pope and James Francis Edward Stuart, son of James II.
1690	At age nineteen, Colley Cibber starts a long theatrical career when he makes his debut as an actor.
1694	Bank of England founded. Queen Mary dies.
1697	Birth of William Hogarth, who will become Britain's leading graphic artist and satirist.
1701	James II dies; his son is proclaimed James III, but only in Paris. A similar effort to proclaim him in London prompts hoots of derision and some street violence.
1702	William III dies; Queen Anne accedes to the throne.
1707	Henry Fielding born 22 April at Sharpham Park, Somerset. His father, Colonel Edmund Fielding, goes off to fight in the War of the Spanish Succession; his mother, Sarah, does not go with her husband. Henry will subsequently have five sisters, a brother, and a half brother. The Act of Union formally unites the governments of Scotland and England, which the English think a good idea.
1710	Fielding's favorite sister, Sarah, born.
1714	Queen Anne, unloved and virtually unmourned, dies without a direct heir, as none of her seventeen children has survived her. The accession of the first of Britain's Hanoverian kings, George I, who prefers Germany and speaks dreadful English, marks the end of the last Tory administration in Fielding's lifetime.

1715	With help from some of the Tory ex-ministers, supporters of "James III" attempt an invasion of Britain. It is a fiasco.
1718	Fielding's mother dies.
1719	Edmund Fielding remarries: Sarah's family is not well pleased; nor do the children take kindly to their stepmother. There is an unholy row and the children are packed off to be educated. The place of torture selected for Henry is Eton.
1720	The South Sea Bubble: people win and lose (mostly lose) fortunes as the stock market crashes, led in its fall by stock in the South Sea Company. Insider dealing had jacked up the price. Robert Walpole forms a new government and is soon known by a new term of abuse: "prime minister."
1725	Jonathan Wild, the most famous criminal of the time, is executed.
1726	Swift's satiric masterpiece, *Gulliver's Travels*, is published.
1727	Accession of George II, who hesitates to reappoint Walpole, but is persuaded to do so by Queen Caroline.
1728	Fielding goes to the Netherlands, apparently to study at Leiden University, but he soon returns to London and writes a vaguely Swiftian poem and a play—an agreeable comedy called *Love in Several Masques*, which his well-connected and influential cousin, Lady Mary Wortley Montagu, helps to get staged. But the unknown playwright must wait, because John Gay's *Beggar's Opera* breaks all box office records and Cibber's *Provok'd Husband* is doing well, too. Their long runs delay Fielding's theatrical debut. Pope's *Dunciad* attracts everyone's attention in the spring.
1729	*A Modest Proposal*, the essay in which Swift ironically suggests that poverty in Ireland can be eradicated if the surplus children are eaten, is published.
1730	Fielding's *Tom Thumb* and *The Author's Farce*, both hilarious comedies, are acted to great applause.
1731	Fielding's new play, *The Grub-Street Opera*, satirizing Walpole and approving of the Opposition led by William Pulteney, is unofficially and illegally censored. Pulteney fights a duel with Lord Hervey over a pamphlet war.
1733	Walpole fails to pass his Excise Bill through Parliament. He is popularly portrayed as a monster trying to overtax and enslave the nation, but nevertheless wins a general election the following year. *The Miser*, Fielding's translation of Molière's *L'Avare*, is a play about money that coincides with the Excise Crisis.

1734	Another hilarious play, *Don Quixote in England,* dedicated to Lord Chesterfield, a prominent Opposition figure, is staged successfully. Fielding marries the beautiful Charlotte Cradock. Over the next eight years, they have three children, who live to be six, eight, and twenty-nine.
1735	In Pope's *Epistle to Dr. Arbuthnot,* Lord Hervey is satirized as Sporus, an obnoxious "thing" of indeterminate sex.
1737	Fielding's plays are getting funnier, wilder, even more popular and more openly hostile to Walpole, whose Licensing Act subjects plays to censorship and is designed to drive Fielding out of the theater. He goes. He becomes a law student. About now, he begins to write *Jonathan Wild,* a novel that satirizes "great men," especially politicians.
1739	With the American émigré James Ralph as co-author, Fielding edits a newspaper, the *Champion.* Britain declares war on Spain. His cousin Lady Mary, who has quarreled with Pope and stood up for Lord Hervey, retires to Italy.
1740	Colley Cibber publishes his sloppily written and amazingly vain autobiography; at age fifty, Samuel Richardson publishes his first novel, *Pamela.* Fielding satirizes both of them.
1741	*The Vernoniad,* a mock-epic in praise of Admiral Vernon's victory over the Spanish at Porto Bello and attacking Walpole for Britain's half-hearted conduct of the war, is published in January. Fielding's imprudent and improvident father dies in June. Fielding meets Ralph Allen and Pope at Allen's new mansion, Prior Park, Bath. Allen will be a firm friend and patron for the rest of their lives. In *The Opposition: A Vision,* published in December, Fielding turns on the people whose politics he has supported for a decade and unexpectedly praises Walpole.
1742	*Joseph Andrews* is published 22 February. Walpole falls after twenty-one consecutive years in power. Fielding is sued for an unpaid debt of £197.
1743	*Miscellanies* published in three volumes 7 April. Volume 3 is *Jonathan Wild.* One of the subscribers is Walpole, who had earlier bribed Fielding, presumably to buy his political support.
1744	Death of his wife, Charlotte, breaks Fielding's heart. Pope dies. Sarah Fielding publishes her first novel, *The Adventures of David Simple.*
1745	Swift dies. The Jacobites, supporters of "James III" (who has lost interest in most things), stage a rebellion led by his son Charles ("Bonny Prince Charlie"). The rebels score some nota-

ble successes, but the uprising is crushed within six months. Fielding edits the *True Patriot*, an anti-Jacobite periodical.

| 1746 | Out of debt at last, he is suddenly plunged right back in it when required to find £400 for a friend's bail. |

1747
Fielding marries his housekeeper, Mary Daniel, to the sneers of the scandalmongers. A son, William, is born the next year, followed by three short-lived girls and a boy, named Allen. Fielding edits the *Jacobite's Journal*, another anti-Jacobite paper.

1748
The seventh and final volume of Richardson's *Clarissa* is published. Fielding admires the novel and writes to Richardson to tell him so. Helped by the influence of John Russell, Duke of Bedford, Fielding becomes a magistrate.

1749
Dedicated to Fielding's lifelong friend George Lyttelton, *Tom Jones* quickly becomes a best-seller to the displeasure of Richardson, who never reads it.

1750
With his blind half-brother and fellow magistrate John ("the blind beak"), Fielding opens an employment agency mainly for people in domestic service.

1751
Tries to devise a way to curb violent street crime in London.

1752
His last novel, *Amelia*, published December 1751, is coolly received. Fielding edits another newspaper, the *Covent-Garden Journal*. With John, founds London's first police force.

1753
Sick, pestered by the Duke of Newcastle, and at four days' notice, Fielding writes a treatise on providing for poor people.

1754
Lady Mary privately condemns his lifelong "indiscretion." In failing health, Fielding travels to Lisbon in the fond belief that its air is unpolluted. Writes an engaging account of the preparations for the journey and of the journey itself. In Lisbon his health does improve but he dies suddenly, aged forty-seven, on 8 October. "No man," writes Lady Mary, "enjoyed life more than he did." Samuel Johnson declares: "he was a blockhead."

1762
Dramatist and journalist Arthur Murphy writes the first biography of Fielding, whose *Works* he edits and publishes, with a frontispiece portrait engraved by Fielding's friend Hogarth.

1764
Ralph Allen dies.

1768
Sarah dies in Richmond, Surrey. She has spent her last years in poverty, helped a little by a one-time grant from the Bath City council. Death of Andrew Millar, Fielding's loyal and generous publisher.

1802
Mary Daniel dies at age eighty-one.

Literary and Historical Context

1

Fielding and His Times

When Sarah Gould Fielding gave birth to her first son on 22 April 1707, her husband, Edmund Fielding, who had just bought a colonelcy, was itching to fight in the War of the Spanish Succession. Britain had been at war for close to twenty years, as part of an untidy mosaic of European efforts to curb French expansionism. But Britain had troubles of her own. In 1688, James II had been deposed; in 1690 the new king, the Dutchman William III, had defeated an army of Irish Catholics at the River Boyne and thereby fanned the flames of an ancient conflict that continues to this day. In 1701 the Act of Settlement ensured that no future monarch would be a Catholic, and in 1707, when Henry Fielding was a month old, Parliament formally united the governments of England and Scotland, alienating many Scots and unintentionally encouraging solidarity among James's supporters. Later, in 1715 and 1745, there were two rebellions aimed at restoring the exiled dynasty.

At the level of everyday life too, Britain could be a turbulent place. London especially experienced a serious and worsening crime rate. Yet despite all the violence and confrontation, Britain was prosperous, elegant, and grand. British society was generally stable, but in another way. What held it together was the emergent culture of capitalism.

As much financial as it was dynastic, the Glorious Revolution of 1688 initiated important changes in British economic and political life. James II had to leave, but there was no coup d'état, no confrontation between Right and Left (the period knew no equivalent of today's Left), no violent overthrow of the ruling class by the underprivileged. Instead, groups whose interests had not been well served arranged a realignment that gave them political rights and a greater share of power. Those same groups rapidly began to develop a larger, more complex, and more sophisticated network of public credit, deficit financing on a grand scale, and rentier income—letting your money earn money—for more individuals than ever before. If we imagine Western capitalism as a high-rise building with ourselves on the top floor, the last quarter of the seventeenth century was the street-level lobby.

To conservative opponents of the economic changes, living on credit was dangerous and the creation of wealth just by moving money around was bewildering. To them the only basis of real wealth was land. Landowners were usually the upper class; that is, the nobility and the aristocracy—recognizable by titles like the Duchess of Lincolnshire or Sir Dennis and Lady Grantham—and some of the gentry—gentlemen, squires, country people whose income came from rent and the profits on farm produce. Landowners had held most of the political power, but now power and prosperity shifted toward bankers, merchants, and shopkeepers. The economic changes (and war loans) meant that the urban middle class, especially, was richer than it had been, and the middle class was growing so fast that it could not be ignored. The financial revolution therefore helped usher in middle class values and tastes.

At this point it becomes necessary to explain what class is. In Britain, unlike the United States, class is not defined by how much money you make. Even if money is relevant, what matters about it is not how much you have but where you get it from and how you spend it. Your place of education—in the sense of the social rather than the intellectual value of the institution—counts for more than money, but what counts most of all is birth: who your parents are, or were. The son of a shopkeeper will always belong to the class of the shopkeeper, though if he becomes a judge, his children will belong to the class of a judge. Class has much to do with perceived status, hierarchy, privilege, exclusiveness, and snobbery.

Fielding's father was more an adventurer than a snob, but he liked to give his children the illusion that they were members of the gentry. The Fieldings and the Goulds had aristocratic pretensions and connections: one of Henry's cousins was the Countess of Denbigh, another was Lady Mary Wortley Montagu, and the Fieldings thought—quite innocently—that they were related to the Habsburgs. Spiritually, if I can put it like that, the Fielding family belonged to the pre-1688 gentry. Materially, they had to earn their income like the rest. Whatever the real or illusory family connections were, Henry Fielding had to earn his living, and he earned it first as the writer of extremely successful plays, then as a lawyer (not a very prosperous one), and lastly as a magistrate who happened to be paid well for his novels. Fielding fended for himself but he was not a self-made man in the sense that his contemporary Samuel Richardson was self-made: Richardson was born with none of Fielding's social advantages, was not "educated" at Eton, was apprenticed to a printer, became a fine printer himself, turned novelist at fifty and was transformed into a reluctant celebrity overnight. From this social point of view, Richardson, rather than Fielding, was the typical writer of the age.

It is harder to say who the typical reader was. For special books published by subscription, we even know the names of the buyers, but, besides inventing this form of the limited edition, the eighteenth-century publishing industry virtually invented the mass market book, a commodity like any other, whose consumers were practically anonymous. No author could neglect the consequences of that anonymity. Some just adopted a commercially successful formula and left it at that, but even the more imaginative writers who went beyond formula still had to consider mass market taste. The taste of the largest group of consumers therefore had a tendency to dictate what was published, as is still the case today. In the eighteenth century that group was the middle class—condemned by its enemies as smug, philistine, and puritanical, an odd combination of assertive self-importance and shy obsequiousness toward the upper class, which the middle class condemned morally but needed materially. The form of literature that appealed more than any other to the middle class was the one that is now dominant: the novel. (Novels also appealed to the upper classes.) No one likes to say just who invented the novel or when, but most people recognize that Daniel Defoe—another self-made man—started the genre on its commercially successful course in 1719 with *Robinson Crusoe*, a classic now, but not then.

Fielding might have read *Crusoe* when he was twelve (though he never mentions it), but he had already read the "real" classics: Homer, Virgil, perhaps Ovid, Livy, and Julius Caesar. He read French and Spanish romances, by Scarron, Cervantes, and the like, history and poetry—but no novels, because when Fielding was a boy, there were none. When Fielding was writing *Joseph Andrews* around 1742, self-appointed arbiters of taste were still reluctant to admit that novels were "literature," perhaps because the genre was new, or because the arbiters did not want to be thought middle class. In any case, the mass market meant that the value of a book could be—crassly—the commercial, not the literary kind. Anyone suspicious of such "values" would be suspicious of the book that was "acclaimed," as we now say ("cried up," they said 250 years ago). And who would be suspicious? Conservatives who resisted or resented the bourgeois revolution.

Readers, sometimes without knowing it, prefer books in which their own views, beliefs, and prejudices are confirmed. A man with roots, real or illusory, in the upper class might well prefer books that confirm the values of that class; a landowner might prefer books that say, in the form of fictional entertainment, that the landowner is the most beneficial member of society. With heroes who are merchants and landowners (Robinson Crusoe is both), eighteenth-century novels often addressed such readers. Fielding wrote novels that tended to entrench conservatism, though in *Joseph Andrews* his characters do not come from the most conservative classes. I do not think he wrote with any narrow class appeal or interest in mind, but in the early 1740s, recently married, forced out of the theater by legislation aimed at silencing his political satire, and desperate for money as usual, Fielding wrote a novel with the obvious hope that it would pay some of his bills.

Fielding was a pragmatist rather than an ideologue. He seems to have cared little for power or its derivatives. He detested pretension, priggishness, and haughtiness, whoever displayed them. He recognized class distinctions and hated the tendency of the middle class to inflate its own importance, but he was much too tolerant to hate the middle class. Besides, he praised the archetypal middle-class creature, the tradesman. Fielding satirized vain people, but his tone was not strident or rancorous: he simply made fun of them. He indulged himself, and us, in laughter at other people's follies, political and otherwise. But Fielding accepted the world as it was, and is: a violent, messy, chaotic, contradictory place.

2

The Importance of the Work

There are, of course, casual readers who check *Joseph Andrews* out of their local public libraries, but today most of the novel's readers are students of English literature. Professors of English, I suspect, would prefer to assign *Tom Jones* but fear that their students will not read such a long book, and so they assign *Joseph Andrews* instead, as if it contained *Tom Jones* in half the space. That is doing some injustice to the author: I doubt that any author sees his earlier work as somehow mere preparation for later fulfillment. Besides, *Joseph Andrews* is not just a shorter *Tom Jones* but a quite different kind of narrative—looser in structure, more vivid in characterization, richer in local color, more intimate, less an object to be admired from a distance. *Tom Jones* is a lot of fun, but it is fun articulated by a grand orchestrator.

Joseph Andrews does not stretch the limits of language as *Ulysses* does, nor does it have the calm assurance of *The Portrait of a Lady*, nor is it universal, haunting, refined, or polished (actually its edges are quite ragged), nor does it even have an especially good or complicated plot. Having said what *Joseph Andrews* is not, I should say what it is and why I think we should read it. This novel may look casual, but it is a carefully constructed romance, which occupies a pivotal place in the history of English fiction; it is a good example of eighteenth-century attitudes to money, morality, politics—to life, in short; it contains one of the most engaging characters in fiction; and most important of all, it is a funny, warm, wise, and humane book. It may be a matter of temperament only, but I can think of no compellingly better reason to read a novel than that it makes me laugh and I learn something from it.

Fielding might never have become a novelist had it not been for two people: Sir Robert Walpole and Samuel Richardson. As prime minister, Walpole was responsible for the Licensing Act, which muted Fielding's political satire and denied him further use of the theater to articulate it. That was in 1737. Fielding then studied law, edited a newspaper, and worked on *Jonathan Wild,* a novel that is a sustained ironic commentary on "great men." The immediate stimulus for *Joseph Andrews* (apart from the need for money) was provided by Richardson's *Pamela,* which appeared in 1740. It is a commonplace of literary history that *Pamela* was the archetypal bourgeois novel. A pretty bad novel but an important document, *Pamela* exemplifies bourgeois morality, is deceptively coy about sex, and shows a servant girl marrying her boss. Middle-class readers seemed to enjoy this fantasy, but Fielding hated it, and parodied *Pamela* in his riotously funny *Shamela. Shamela* is only a fifty-page booklet, but Fielding crammed a lot of satire into it. Although Richardson's novel is *Shamela's* main target, Fielding also satirized Colley Cibber, the leading playwright of the day (Fielding was second only to him in London's theatrical world), vain man, and author of a badly written autobiography that also came out in 1740; Conyers Middleton, biographer of Cicero, whose main crime seems to have been dedicating his book to Lord Hervey; and Lord Hervey himself, an effeminate, bisexual courtier, apologist for Walpole's administration, friend of Fielding's cousin Lady Mary Wortley Montagu (but she was living in Italy by this time), and mortal enemy of Pope, who put every one of these people in that catalog of the small and evil, the *Dunciad.* Fielding also had a few shots at the clergy, politicians, and other hypocrites.

It always seems hard in general to discuss Fielding and

Richardson without reference to each other because they gave the genre of the novel the two main streams of its subsequent course. And although it seems hard in particular to discuss *Joseph Andrews* without *Pamela*, Fielding's novel is neither a continuation of *Shamela* nor just another parody of *Pamela*. In *Joseph Andrews*, Fielding mocks *Pamela* certainly, repeats some of the same concerns and satirizes the same people. Yet he did much more at the same time: he mocked the entire basis, which I call a class basis, on which *Pamela* was constructed. I think *Joseph Andrews* is among other things a satire of bourgeois mentality. Many critics would disagree with me; an especially large number of them would stress this novel's comic, as opposed to its satiric, elements.

Whatever the extent of the satire, *Joseph Andrews* is more than merely Fielding's response to people and concepts he disliked. It is an affirmation of its author's values in a bourgeois milieu that, as I said in chapter 1, was paradoxically turbulent and stable. Fielding approved of benevolence: in a culture governed by money and greed, all too often disguised by a veil of hypocritical morality, there was, he hoped, room for a truly kind-hearted, good-natured man. The "good" characters in Fielding novels are spontaneous, generous, willing to share whatever they have with people who are less fortunate; they are also natural, unaffected, incapable of putting on airs.

The eighteenth century is really the last period to receive new and invigorating critical and historical treatment in our time. The popular image of the period in Britain is changing: it used to be characterized, in history and criticism, as gentlemanly and decorous, full of powdered wigs and courteous bowing, politicians discussing matters of state in dignified surroundings with a good deal of ceremony, well-dressed ladies and gentlemen dancing minuets. In spite of the counter-evidence offered by Hogarth's and then Rowlandson's graphic satires, the period came across as elegant, a bit stuffy and rather boring. Now, more emphasis is being given to the seamier realities of political corruption, greed and self-serving, and also to the utterly unglamorous aspects of everyday life: the filth and disease, poverty, misery, and crime.

The Importance of the Work

Once these aspects of British culture are uncovered, Fielding's place in the period becomes more interesting. He was a gentleman hack writer, a paradox in our time perhaps, but not in his. Continually in debt, a self-appointed watchdog of political chicanery, or what would now be called sleaze, Fielding recognized dirt and danger, lust and violence, and in his late years as a magistrate came face to face with the hopeless world of the disadvantaged, the criminals, the victims, and the wretched. All this experience went into his novels, as well as into his essays on social problems.

With the exception of *Amelia*, Fielding's novels are not outspoken protests; instead they tend to idealize the poor or disenfranchised, highlighting their problems but then solving them with a wave of the magic wand. A poor man turns out to be rich, an abandoned bastard turns out to have been born a gentleman: Fielding's solutions to real material problems belong to romance rather than to the real world. In socioeconomic terms therefore, Fielding's novels are finally fantastic, and so radical readers today often find him too conservative to interest them, which may only mean that they are dismissing someone because he does not tell them what they want to hear. But at the same time his novels have a kind of documentary function because they reveal so much of what was, to Fielding, everyday life.

3

Critical Reception

Fielding's reputation is somewhat unusual in that there is a whole book devoted to it: F. T. Blanchard's *Fielding the Novelist: A Study in Historical Criticism.* Tracing the changing reception of Fielding's fiction from mid-eighteenth-century hostility to Victorian censoriousness to early twentieth-century admiration, Blanchard established many interesting points, including these: *Joseph Andrews* was eventually as popular as *Tom Jones;*[1] in the nineteenth century it took someone as formidably influential as Samuel Taylor Coleridge to rehabilitate Fielding when he had been dismissed for years as a lightweight, "a 'wit,' a writer of 'facetious memory'";[2] Fielding's reading public was loyal (before *Amelia*), although critics by and large were not.[3] In his own lifetime, Fielding enjoyed popular success, not critical acclaim. He himself preferred *Joseph Andrews* to his other writings—though he said so before he had written *Tom Jones* and *Amelia*[4]—but it was a long time before his first novel was widely appreciated.

In the preface to *Joseph Andrews,* Fielding makes what looks like a statement of his objectives. It turns out to be a critical smokescreen, as he seems to say first that *Joseph Andrews* is a romance, and then that it is neither a romance nor a burlesque but a comic romance, or a "hitherto unattempted" English comic prose epic. Many a critic has tried to determine what Fielding really meant by this, and since I have commented on that elsewhere,[5] I will not repeat myself here; but I would emphasize that Fielding's assured tone is probably not serious, so that whatever he is saying about comic prose epics, we might do well to listen to the way he is saying it—with a poker face. Fielding's earliest readers did not have much trouble recognizing his ironic humor, even if many of them did not like it.

It is much easier to extract from that preface Fielding's intention to expose vanity, affectation, flattery, and hypocrisy. He does expose these traits in the course of the novel, but the exposure is not what early readers generally found most interesting or valuable about it. In the middle of the eighteenth century no newspapers and only a few magazines printed reviews, so that many of the very earliest responses have to be gleaned from private correspondence. In Fielding's own time, comments, private or published, about *Joseph Andrews* are surprisingly scarce: not quite the virtual silence of which Blanchard speaks, but still amounting only to about two dozen items (some just passing comments) in another useful source, *Henry Fielding: The Critical Heritage.*

Fielding would not have been encouraged if he had known that the poet William Shenstone found the character of Parson Adams "tedious,"[6] or that Andrew Ramsay found *Joseph Andrews* so dull that he gave up after reading only half of it.[7] Dr. George Cheyne (whom Fielding had satirized in 1740 for his eccentric English, but not for the usual reasons—Cheyne's notorious 450-pound weight, and his being a doctor) condemned the novel as fit only for "Porters or Watermen,"[8] which presumably means it was not intellectual enough for his taste. The earliest approval of the novel seems to have come from Elizabeth Carter, the bluestocking, who found it "perfectly agreeable entertainment," which she praised for "such a surprising variety of nature, wit, morality, and good sense, as is scarcely to be met with in any one composition," the whole novel being "peculiarly charming" on account of its "spirit of benevolence." Carter recognized and approved of the satire "and yet" she had "met with some people who treat it in the most outrageous manner."[9] She saw the novel as moral, but others drew the opposite conclusion.

The first "rave" review came from the Abbé Desfontaines, who admired *Joseph Andrews* enormously, praised Fielding's comic skills extravagantly, and then translated the novel into French in 1743. Desfontaines's introduction to his translation highlighted other aspects of the novel than comic technique; he told his reader:

> You will judge his skill in this genre by a large number of features prevalent in his book, and especially by the dialogues, for which he possesses talent of the highest order. But you will value most highly the honesty of all his descriptions and of all his expressions, and the wisdom with which he treats a subject which could have drawn him into licentious descriptions. . . . Should some critic find some basic fault in this excellent fiction, which is the love of a lady for her servant whom she has considered marrying, a thought which she nevertheless condemns and never executes, I would ask him if the history of Potiphar's wife with regard to the young Joseph of the Scriptures, injures his sense of decency.[10]

There is much more in this vein; the whole introduction is well worth reading for its common sense and critical intelligence. The translation itself was good, too, and gave Fielding a fairly enthusiastic French readership. Translations into other languages quickly followed, as did four more editions in England. These facts suggest considerable demand for *Joseph Andrews*. In its first year in England, 6,500 copies had been printed (at a time when a best-seller would run to 10,000 or more), 2,000 more were printed in 1748, and another 2,000 in 1749, soon after *Tom Jones* was published.[11] It often happens that a best-seller impels readers to look for the author's earlier books, and so it was with Fielding: *Joseph Andrews* attracted more critical attention once *Tom Jones* proved to be a tremendous success. In the absence of very much published critical comment that could have prompted or inhibited sales, our obvious conclusion has to be that for the first five years readers were privately recommending *Joseph Andrews* to their friends and acquaintances. The novel seems to have continued to evoke this mixture of responses—lavish praise, outright condemnation; popular interest, critical reserve—for most of the eighteenth century.

The critical reception of *Joseph Andrews*, then, was a bit sparse to begin with, and subsequently somewhat mixed. In 1762, Arthur Murphy certainly helped to improve Fielding's reputation in general with a biographical and critical essay designed to establish Fielding as a comic genius and *Joseph Andrews* as "the sun-rise of our author's genius."[12] Murphy praised this novel for its comedy, organization, and invention, and for "the humanity, and benevolence of affection, the goodness of heart, and the zeal for virtue," which are expressed in the character of Parson Adams.[13] The "unabating pleasantry" with which the novel is "sustained" was, said Murphy, "sufficiently felt and acknowledged."[14]

Eighteenth-century readers typically responded to Fielding's humor and to his morality or immorality. *Tom Jones* generated more such responses than *Joseph Andrews*, but those responses were quickly applied to Fielding personally and thus to all his works. Readers also continually tried to locate the original models for Fielding's characters, particularly Parson Adams. It was quite common then to think of characters as being real people in disguise, whereas now we are more likely to think of them as products of an artist's imagination, based on real people but not slavishly describing them. Disappointed by the characters in *Tom Jones*, Shenstone came to think that Parson Adams—whoever he might be based on—was the redeeming feature of *Joseph Andrews*: "an original . . . unattempted before, & yet so natural yt most people seem'd to know ye Man."[15] The real person behind Adams was in fact an eccentric clergyman and friend of the author's, William Young, but two disapproving critics did not actually know that. One of them, Francis Coventry, noted that *Joseph Andrews* was a novel of real life because the characters were drawn from real people, and then he dismissed the "story" as "dull."[16] The other, Samuel Richardson, dismissed all Fielding's novels, saying that they were so low the author must have been born in a stable,[17] and he condemned them for lacking inventiveness precisely because the characters were not (he alleged) the products of Fielding's imagination, but "mere" portraits of himself, his family, and his friends.[18] To a great extent, Richardson's hostility to Fielding was a result of envy: he was jealous of Fielding's success with *Tom Jones,* which he never even read.

While both men were still alive, it became standard critical procedure to treat Fielding and Richardson together, to play each one off the other, and Fielding's reputation suffered because eighteenth- and nineteenth-century taste preferred Richardson's "fine sentiments" to Fielding's "low humour." Readers who are not critics apparently see no need to indulge in the comparison game, but for over two centuries the pundits have contrasted Fielding's immorality and Richardson's morality, Fielding's lightness (or superficiality) and Richardson's seriousness, Fielding's bawdy comedy and Richardson's lofty tragedy. Even for those denying that Fielding is immoral, light, or "low," the contrast with Richardson still comes in handy. The contrast originated because the two men invited it: Fielding parodied Richardson's *Pamela* with his own *Shamela; Joseph Andrews* was at least in part a response to *Pamela* too; Fielding's comic epic, *Tom Jones,* was published so soon after Richardson's tragic one, *Clarissa,* that comparison was inevitable (and, in a late chapter of *Tom Jones,* Fielding says as much); and Richardson and his circle of worshipers sneered at Fielding's fiction. They were rivals in almost everyone's eyes. Readers seem to have found it difficult to like both of them.

The contrast with Richardson still thrives (like dozens of other professors, I use it myself in the classroom), but now the original estimates of the value or importance of the two novelists have undergone radical change. Fielding is no longer scorned for his alleged immorality, and the charge of "lowness"—which really tells us that Fielding wrote about ordinary people without covering up such basic human traits as appetites—has slipped into the half-light of critical irrelevance. Most significantly perhaps, twentieth-century critics have found something sinister, perhaps even voyeuristic, in Richardson's claustrophobic fiction of attempted assault on the virgin purity of his heroine, Clarissa, whose status has been elevated almost to the mythic. Richardson's fictions have come to be virtual definitions of what is most important and revealing about eighteenth-century culture. There is nothing wrong with that. At the same time, critics (rarely the same ones who write about Richardson) have Christianized Fielding. Both authors are now considered "important," whatever that may mean, though if Richardson's immense achievement is perhaps thought to be the more worthy of serious consideration, I suspect that may be because academic critics value tragedy above comedy.

Wilbur Cross in 1918 and James A. Work in 1949 both did much to clear away the popular image of Fielding as a dissolute rake who therefore must have written dissolute books.[19] Cross's laudatory biography and Work's brief, sober analysis of Fielding's journalism (mainly) showed that Fielding and his mature works were capable of interpretation based on perfectly serious religious content. It is a mystery to me that the blatant religious content of *Joseph Andrews,* in particular, could ever have been missed, but it attracted virtually no notice until the appearance in 1959 of Martin C. Battestin's important and influential critical study.[20] Recognizing of course that Parson Adams has plenty to say about religion, Battestin traced many of Fielding's religious views to a doctrine so broad, so loose, and ultimately so undoctrinaire that it is very difficult to define: it was known as latitudinarianism, signifying latitude in matters of religion. With a paradoxical irony that would surely have amused Fielding, thirty scholars at a recent conference in Los Angeles snarled at each other for days about precisely what constitutes latitudinarianism. Seen in the light of the sermons of the leading latitudinarian divines, along with Fielding's many personal adaptations and additions, *Joseph Andrews,* Battestin showed, is a serious novel with a considerable religious dimension.

Although many subsequent critics have found Fielding's importance in quite different aspects of *Joseph Andrews* (and the other novels), only one, Arthur Sherbo, has seriously challenged Battestin's case, but he has won no support.[21] Some critics think Battestin's argument makes Fielding seem solemn or dull, which most of us (including Battestin) think he is not. Others take the argument to mean that Fielding's main subject is Christian morality, an implication that is challenged when, for instance, Ronald Paulson states in an introduction to a brief critical anthology on Fielding "that the subject matter of Fielding's best work is not the medicine of Christian morality but the disease for which it may be prescribed."[22] Fielding had already anticipated this objection in his preface to *Joseph Andrews* when he noted that in his novel there are lots of vices because they are inescapable in any "Series of human Actions," but that they are "never . . . the Objects of Ridicule but of Detestation," that they do not dominate any scene in which they occur, and that "they never produce the intended Evil."[23] To cut a long argument short, if we follow Paulson's line of thought we are more likely to judge that Fielding's mode is primarily satiric, while Battestin's approach tends to the view that Fielding is primarily comic.[24]

It is a real tribute to Battestin that Fielding's moral seriousness seems to be assured, but that is of course not the final critical word on his novels. Numerous other aspects of Fielding's writing have been scrutinized, especially his conscious artifice, his narrative technique, his irony, his characterization, and the degree of realism in his novels, which critics collectively portray as confirmations of civilized social structures or harmonious ideals. All this is both welcome and debatable, but hardly exhaustive. Fielding's novels have not yet been approached rigorously by feminists, deconstructionists, or Marxists. The received critical opinion of Fielding has been fashioned by male traditionalists.[25] It is only a matter of time before Fielding's fiction is shown to be patronizing in its attitudes to women, or marginal to what someone takes to be the main concerns of eighteenth-century life and literature, but I leave these important and worthwhile tasks to others to perform.

My discussion of *Joseph Andrews* is meant to cover neither every critical angle nor every aspect of the novel. My approach to *Joseph Andrews* is historical: I do not mean by this that I am tracking down the significance of Fielding's topical allusions, but that I treat this novel as a product (whether central or marginal is not the point) of its time and a commentary on it. The main concerns of that period, like those of most periods, revolved around money and power (or, for many people, poverty and impotence), with the difference in the eighteenth century that the distribution of these two commodities was changing into a pattern that, more or less, is with us today. These concerns affected virtually every aspect of the culture, which happens to have been predominantly bourgeois, and so I am treating *Joseph Andrews* as a novel that responds to middle-class attitudes (on a wide range of issues) that a gentleman such as Fielding could have encountered every day.[26] The issues are quite familiar: sex, violence, morality, hypocrisy, vanity, hierarchy, money, and class. *Joseph Andrews* is certainly topical, but it is not necessary to have a history degree to understand it today.

A Reading

4

Objects of Satire

Satire and comedy are easily confused. Because we are always told in textbooks and glossaries that satire diminishes its object by ridicule, we usually think of satire as funny. And because we usually associate "funny" with comedy, it follows that satire and comedy must be similar, if not the same. It would be more accurate to say that comedy is happy rather than funny, and that some satire can be funny. *As You Like It* is less funny than it is happy, but it is still a comedy; the Earl of Rochester's satires, such as "A Ramble in St. James's Park," are violent and degrading, not funny, but they are still satires. Fielding is the kind of writer who causes us very easily to merge comedy and satire until they become a blur in our minds. His novels, and *Joseph Andrews* in particular, satirize various people and types of behavior: he laughs at them, and invites us to share in the laughter. His novels also end happily, and they are funny, so that however we define comedy we would probably think of *Joseph Andrews* as a comic novel, which also satirizes—that is, which diminishes a subject by ridicule.[27]

I have used this difficult, often hazy distinction between these two literary cousins, satire and comedy, not because I want to pursue questions of mode and which one *Joseph Andrews* exploits, but because it is a means of investigating the tone of this novel. There was something steely and dangerous and menacing about Swift and his satire, something violent and angry about Rochester and his. I would be terrified to have Swift as a guest for dinner, but I would have no hesitation in inviting Fielding, because he never had Swift's capacity for rage. Both men detested hypocrisy, but while Swift would metaphorically flay a hypocrite, Fielding would just show us the hypocrite's absurdity. It is as if Swift would go for the jugular but Fielding would see the funny side, shrug, and call for another bottle of wine. The purpose of satire for Swift and Fielding alike was ultimately moral. The commonplace definitions of the day all sounded something like Dryden's: "The true end of *Satyre*, is the amendment of Vices by correction."[28] Fielding did see that there was a funny side to hypocrisy, but that does not mean he considered hypocrisy to be unimportant or that he took it lightly, and yet it seems to be one of the hazards of comic writing that it is not taken seriously, and Fielding's tone has caused his novels to be condemned as trivial.

In the preface to *Joseph Andrews,* Fielding announces that the ridiculous is his province. He then names affectation as "The only Source of the true Ridiculous," and so diverts our attention toward rather silly behavior, such as putting on airs, being pretentious, trying to look and sound important—the sort of thing we all recognize in any society where posing is common. No one in his right mind would consider the poseur as a threat to society, nor does Fielding, but he does say that what lies behind affectation is something that can be much more serious, for "Affectation proceeds from one of these two Causes, Vanity, or Hypocrisy" (8; preface). These, especially hypocrisy, are the targets of his satire. Affectation in itself may be harmless, but if it arises from hypocrisy it points to a serious flaw in a person, and one that may hurt other people. A satirist can either declare war on affected people or point at them and laugh. Fielding thought the latter was more likely than the former to persuade people to recognize their own weaknesses, but he was also enough of a realist to know that satirists do not address their victims directly. As Swift had said, definitively, in 1704, "*Satyr is a sort of* Glass, *wherein Beholders do generally discover every body's Face but their Own.*"[29] Making fun of vain and affected people is therefore part of a campaign to expose a serious social ill, but only an optimist would believe that an affected person changes his ways because he reads about himself. Satirists therefore have only a slim chance of being successful social reformers.

In satirizing anyone at all, Fielding was addressing those people who already recognized the things he was exposing. It is still true, too: we can all (I presume) recognize the shyster lawyer, or the doctor who keeps us waiting—which all doctors do as a matter of course—but do lawyers or doctors read *Joseph Andrews,* and if so, would they see themselves there? Swift knew they would not and, given the nature of the satire in *Joseph Andrews,* Fielding knew it too. Even though Fielding was preaching to the converted, he was exposing something that of itself did not need exposing, because it was already obvious. His satire therefore might have tended to have the effect of encouraging a kind of solidarity: "we" recognize what the satirist points out, so "we" are separate from the ridiculous people, who are "them." Right away we know we have a divided society—in this case the affected (or vain, or hypocritical) and the natural (or straightforward, or honest). That function of Fielding's satire is important, for reasons I will explore later. Also, the satire encourages another, different kind of solidarity, between author and reader, so that if the author laughs, the reader is encouraged to laugh with him—and that may persuade us to think of the satire as if it were comedy. Perhaps most revealing of all about this satire of the obvious is that it would be pointless to satirize vanity unless your readers thought there was a lot of vanity around, and similarly with hypocrisy, affectation, and so on. These characteristics have to be commonplace; otherwise the satirist seems to be wasting his time and energy on trivia. Underlying the very obviousness of the satiric targets, therefore, is a presumed sense of truth—that this is the way the world is (and perhaps always was).

Hypocrisy and vanity have surely existed for as long as "civilization" has and lawyers have probably always behaved in the ways that satirists suggest they have. These are two implications of Fielding's comments at the beginning of book 3 when he states the satirist's usual claim to "describe not Men, but Manners; not an Individual, but a Species . . . the Lawyer is not only alive, but hath been so these 4000 Years. . . . He hath not indeed confined himself to one Profession, one Religion, or one Country; but when the first mean selfish Creature appeared on the human Stage, who made Self the Centre of the whole Creation; would give himself no Pain, incur no Danger, advance no Money to assist, or preserve his Fellow-Creatures; then was our Lawyer born; and whilst such a Person as I have described, exists on Earth, so long shall he remain upon it" (189; 3, 1). Fielding advertises his intention to satirize the vices, but one specific vice, greed for money, can exist only in a society that places high value on money. Ancient Sparta, for instance, where the currency was large iron bars rather than gold or silver, would not have been a very plausible place for a satirist to look for misers to expose, because a miser would have needed a warehouse to store his wealth. The particular combination that Fielding satirizes in *Joseph Andrews* is hypocrisy, vanity, affectation, snobbishness, lust, and material greed. Each of these traits individually is very common, and certainly not limited to a particular society. The combination had been visible in other cultures at other times (Rome in the first century A.D., for example), and is still alive and well in the Western world today. It is a combination that tells us something about the configuration of a society—English society of the mid-eighteenth century or any society that resembles it.

The main satiric target of *Joseph Andrews* is hypocrisy, as the preface promises. Parson Barnabas, Parson Trulliber, Lady Booby, and many other characters behave in ways that belie their motives, which is the basis of hypocrisy. To cite just one small and fairly obvious example, Lady Booby "plainly saw the Effects which Town-Air hath on the soberest Constitutions. She would now walk out with [Joseph] into *Hyde-Park* in a Morning, and when tired, which happened almost every Minute, would lean on his Arm, and converse with him in great Familiarity" (27; 1, 4). It does not take a genius to see that Lady Booby is not in the least interested in the effects of the town air, nor is she truly tired. The description is good basic comedy, and no doubt most readers laugh or smile at it, but her behavior—without being outrageous or shocking—is still hypocritical.

Fielding's usual satiric tone is similarly ironic: "His [Parson Adams's] Virtue and his other Qualifications, as they rendered him equal to his Office, so they made him an agreeable and valuable Companion, and had so much endeared and well recommended him to a Bishop, that at the Age of Fifty, he was provided with a handsome Income of twenty-three Pounds a Year" (23; 1, 3). At the time Fielding was writing, an income of £23 a year was very far from "handsome," as in fact he goes on to hint. The burden of the paragraph is to recommend Parson Adams to us, but one of the effects introduced by Fielding is to satirize "a Bishop," and so really the church hierarchy for underpaying their ordinary clergymen. Elsewhere in the novel there are more direct attacks on corruption in the clergy, but here the satire is smuggled in. Once we as readers are accustomed to this ironic tone, which is actually the norm for the novel, we recognize the point of the satire. Another early example concerns the nominal "hero," Joseph. As Lady Booby's footman, Joseph is supposed to attend her in public, "and when he attended his Lady at Church (which was but seldom) he behaved with less seeming Devotion than formerly" (27; 1, 4). The minuscule satiric barb here is not directed at Joseph for lack of "seeming devotion" to his mistress, but at Lady Booby herself, whose lack of "devotion" in another sense is made evident by the fact that she rarely goes to church. This therefore is another instance of her hypocrisy.

It is important for the tone of the novel that such small instances as these could occur early in the narrative, as indeed they do, a whole cluster of them. Sir Thomas Booby dies in a subordinate clause, so that we know, before we actually get to the narrator's explanation, that "his disconsolate Lady" is not disconsolate at all, but pleased to have got rid of her husband. She is "confined to her House as closely as if she herself had been attacked by some violent Disease" (28–29; 1, 5). Fielding's phrasing borders on the miraculous. We know that Lady Booby is utterly self-centered without his having to tell us so, and when in the next chapter Joseph spells it all out, that Lady Booby never loved her husband and always quarreled with him, the net effect is that we recognize Joseph's naïveté as he says "if it had not been so great a Lady, I should have thought she had a mind to me," which of course she does because she is driven by sexual desire for Joseph. Lady Booby's behavior is therefore fundamentally hypocritical (as it will continue to be), but I think we can learn much more from listening to the satirist's tone of voice, that is, from listening to *how* he says something rather than only to *what* he says.

Hypocrisy, of course, is a matter of disguising real motives. Lady Booby disguises hers continually. We see her game easily, but Joseph does not. The main result of this contrast is basically funny: his innocence is absurd when he is apparently blissfully unaware that his employer is lusting after him all the time. But the contrast is instructive, too. The whole narrative proper begins with one of Fielding's almost proverbial observations: "It is a trite but true Observation, that Examples work more forcibly on the Mind than Precepts" (17; 1, 1). In the chapter that follows this remark, he emphasizes the idea that the "lives" of his characters are indeed exemplary. This all seems to mean that the characters are more important for the traits they exemplify than for the personalities they might be supposed to have. What they stand for in the fiction is what counts. Lady Booby's comic behavior, like Joseph's equally comic stoic resistance to her seduction, matters more than her, or his, personality. The characters are not developed, of course. Out of the comic clash of the two characters emerges a satiric wit that plays off desire against innocence, or rather, the power of lust against the power of love. The force of lustful desire is associated with the hypocrite, and so we easily recognize that lust is associated with falsity, disguise, and deceit. If the satire works at all, it does so at this level of assembling a composite image of other traits besides hypocrisy and lumping them all together. By contrast, Joseph, although unlikely to convince any of us that his is the way to live, emerges as honest, likable, and innocent. What we are seeing is a contrast between two exemplary characters—that is, two characters who are examples of particular facets of human nature. Since the characters are not much more than vehicles for those traits, the satire gives body to abstractions in this way, and also tells us that what Fielding has to say is essentially moral.

The fact remains that most of us are more likely than not to laugh at all this. Joseph Andrews may be a paragon of innocence, and there is nothing intrinsically funny about innocence, but I laugh at him. And Slipslop, who emulates her mistress, is no less absurd. If Slipslop is risible, it is (I hope) because she is incongruous rather than because we find the sexual passion of an ugly postmenopausal woman funny. This unlovely character is an object of satire, to be sure, and she is driven by the same sexual urges as Lady Booby, though she has a much more remote chance of success because of her age and ugliness. But Slipslop is also the subject of moral commentary not only because of the parallel with Lady Booby but because she is vain yet has so little to be vain about. When her temper is "a little softened" by Joseph's "Compliment to her Learning," it is her vanity, not her learning, that Fielding satirizes (33; 1, 6).

The novel's satire is perhaps at its most conspicuously moral in the famous scene involving the stagecoach passengers and their reactions when they come across Joseph, who has been robbed, stripped, and beaten by a gang of thieves (52–55; 1, 12). The postilion, with highly questionable logic, thinks the man they have come across must be dead because they can hear him groan. The satire begins then with the coachman wanting to hurry on by; a lady wants to hurry away, too, because Joseph is naked (she has not a thought for his condition). Hearing that Joseph has been robbed, a gentleman wants to leave for fear he may be robbed, and a lawyer wishes they had gone past already because they might be answerable if Joseph dies. Every one of these people after the postilion is concerned only with his or her own interest. None of them has a word to say about the "poor Wretch" except as he might affect their self-interest. The remainder of the scene elaborates on these attitudes. Only the postilion shows any charity and common decency toward Joseph, and he gives the poor fellow his coat. We learn that the postilion "hath been since transported for robbing a Hen-roost," but the real crime here is the callous selfishness of the others. It is not the occurrence of crime that occupies Fielding's attention, or ours, but the sanctimonious hypocrisy that it provokes among the well-to-do.

As we approach the end of book 1, we have read several examples of hypocritical behavior, and it is clear which side the author is on, which side he is inviting us to join. What the satirist has been doing is to enlist our support, so to speak, in seeing that Lady Booby is hypocritical in not even caring about her husband's death, and that Parson Barnabas has no interest in religion (even though it is meant to be his job), that he prefers material over spiritual matters (58–59; 1, 13), and that the surgeon will do his job only at his own convenience unless there is someone rich to be milked (55; 1, 12). As examples like these accumulate, we are likely to come ever closer to adopting the satirist's point of view on a wide range of issues. If he uses the same technique, the same kind of ironies, the same tone, the same smuggling in of little hints that dispose us to notice and judge his characters, then he can start to exploit us, for whatever purpose he chooses. And I suggest that he does, again in small ways.

There is no reason to suppose that everyone thinks that charity is a good or desirable thing. Plenty of people do not like charity, for one reason or another, and some of those people read Fielding's novel. But if Fielding, who thought charity is important, could get us laughing with him, and could smuggle charity into his text in the same way that he worked in Lady Booby's hypocrisy, he would have a chance of persuading some of those readers to agree with him. The hideous and parsimonious Mrs. Tow-wouse (whose name itself is an obscenity) is no ambassador for anything at all, and so when she shouts, "Common Charity, a F--t!" Fielding aligns an obnoxious woman with what is (to him) an obnoxious opinion. If we dislike her, we will (perhaps) be more likely to dislike what she says and what, as an exemplary character, she stands for. The novel is full of other exemplary characters (Leonora, one host, Wilson, Leonard and Paul) who function in the same way.

I am concentrating on the technique rather than the substance of Fielding's satire, partly because the substance is fairly obvious, and partly because the technique suggests a pattern. Everything has an explanation in a Fielding novel. For instance, Slipslop's amazing failure to recognize Fanny, whom she knows perfectly well, is explained (158; 2, 13), and her subsequent ill-tempered refusal to allow Fanny "or any such Trollops" to enter her company is explained not as sudden snobbishness but as a desire to get rid of Fanny so that she (Slipslop) can sink her claws into Joseph (159; 2, 13). Things that are puzzling turn out to have a reason, which the author usually provides, and the reason, repeatedly, is self-interest, whether sexual, financial, or political.

Even in small ways and trivial cases, self-interest dominates the behavior of the characters. The first would-be seducer/rapist we meet "had a Readiness at improving any Accident," and so accuses Adams (with grotesque injustice and untruth) of robbery: he has his eyes on a reward, of course (141–42; 2, 10). In the subsequent scene, the local parson pretends to understand Greek so as to cut an impressive figure in front of the even more thunderingly ignorant local magistrate and the crowd of bird batters whose sport it is to arrest Adams in the first place (148–49; 2, 11). These are minor instances of self-interest, expressed in mild ways, but they are common throughout the novel (e.g., the poet and the player in 3, 12). The more substantial ones have to do with money, security, and power. Trulliber's nastiness in refusing to lend Adams any money is not only a satire on those corrupt clergymen who earned the church a bad name, but also an indication of a coarse boorish bully who treats his cowed wife with brutal contempt and whose overriding interest is money (166–67; 2, 14). Peter Pounce devotes his life to money, particularly other people's.

Self-interest is obviously not restricted to any particular society or period of history. It may be more prominent or common at one time than another, but it is plainly a common human characteristic. What I call the politics of interest is less conspicuous. Self-advancement in eighteenth-century England was difficult without contacts, as it still is today in most professional fields. Now it is called networking and usually (we like to think) does not involve bribery; then it was called corruption and did. The system involved what is known in some parts of the world as baksheesh: to get a better job, or to get a job at all, meant approaching someone with power over the job, and paying him (or, occasionally, her) to take you into consideration. In effect, this entailed bribing a sequence of people in order to have your name—if you were lucky—included with other applicants. Sir Robert Walpole ran the government of the country on a principle of bribery and corruption and boasted about the success of his system. In Fielding's novel, this need for "interest" occurs numerous times, and acts as a kind of backdrop to the actions of the characters, such as Adams's account of how pressure was put on him to secure a vote for a politician (132–34; 2, 8). Fielding mentions in passing that Joseph did not attend a charity school, because "his Father . . . had not Interest enough to get him into" one (24; 1, 3). Two paragraphs later, we learn that Adams has access to Lady Booby only "through the Waiting-Gentlewoman," Mrs. Slipslop. Adams is dependent on Sir Thomas (and what an unpleasant man *he* is) and Lady Booby: to keep even his wretched position he must have "interest" with them. There are indications of hierarchy everywhere, from the "Ladder of Dependance" to Lady Booby's roller coaster passion for Joseph, which is continually modified when she remembers that he is her servant (36; 1, 7). All this spills over into flattery of the powerful and rich, contempt for the weak and poor (e.g., 99; 2, 3). Mrs. Slipslop is typical of many of Fielding's characters who make the mistake of thinking that being haughty to her "inferiors" is a sign of her own importance and will be read as one by her own "superiors." The truth is that Mrs. Slipslop is indispensable to Lady Booby, who in turn holds her in contempt.

Lady Booby is the most socially elevated character in the novel, and so in a sense does not need to impress anyone, yet she has eyes for one of the socially lowest, Joseph Andrews. Early in the novel, the narrator speaks of Lady Booby as "the Heroine of our Tale" (38; 1, 8), which of course she is not, any more than Joseph is its hero. Joseph Andrews is not a particularly interesting character, nor even, oddly enough, a very important one. The protagonist of the novel is actually Parson Adams. But Joseph's role is important, and so is his virtue. With no innocent man, there would be no comic exposure of Lady Booby's lust, and with no faithful lover, there could be no contrast with the continual predatory schemes of lustful men trying to rape Fanny. The fiction's basic arrangement is therefore a pattern of innocence and virtue falling prey to lust and hypocrisy, again and again. One might ask why there are so many conflicts that are barely more than variations on this one central clash. I suspect that there are two probable answers. The first answer, which is also the simpler one, is that hypocrisy and vanity are widespread human traits and the sooner we admit this, the better, because we would then be in a stronger position to recognize them and defend ourselves against them. Such thinking would be in keeping also with Fielding's ideas in his other writings. The second, slightly more complex answer is that the motives of the predators are always governed by self-interest. People think they will get somewhere, gain something, if they act falsely and impose upon the innocent. And the fact is that they do gain something, usually money.

Fielding's satire projects a world in which people who have principles are, to put it mildly, extremely rare. In this novel there are possibly five characters who do: Fanny, Joseph, Adams, the pedlar, and Wilson. Wilson is a reformed rake, Fanny says too little for us to form much judgment about her principles, the pedlar performs one charitable act but is necessary for the resolution of the plot, and so we are left with Joseph and Adams. Adams, the most principled of them all, is also the most unworldly, the most naive. But of all the instances of either his naïveté or his principles, one, surprisingly, is overlooked by most commentators and critics. This is the story he tells of how he lost his curacy because he would not bow to political pressure (132– 33; 2, 8). This is not so much unworldliness as a stubborn refusal to be compromised: "I am an honest Man, and would not do an ill Thing to be made a Bishop," says Adams, but when the man whose interest Adams had supported abandons him, his surprise does sound like naïveté (133; 2, 8). When you expect people to keep their promises because you keep your own, you are in a fantasy world, and so the narrator can say with some justice that Adams's "Discourse . . . is not only the most curious in this, but perhaps in any other Book" (132; 2, 8, chapter heading). For this is an example of what I take to be the drift of all the satire of *Joseph Andrews:* it matters that vanity and hypocrisy are exposed, but it matters far more that they are seen to be so pervasive. Adams's naïveté is not an alternative or an antidote to them, exactly, but rather his principles, admirable as they are, do not work in a world that is dominated by corrupt self-interest and desire for money. The novel was written during a phase of capitalism (in the guise of limited democracy) that pushed corruption, self-interest, and money into the limelight. The moral purpose of Fielding's satire was, if nothing else, timely.

5

H*umor*

Some readers find Fielding's humor heavy-handed. Fair enough; sometimes it is laborious. Fielding is not usually the subtlest of ironists, as even his most ardent champions would probably concede. And the intrusive narrator who explains some of his witticisms does take some getting used to. The ethos of Fielding's narratives depends partly on shared humor (or more generally, a sort of seeing eye to eye with his reader), and that means that the narrator continually offers us his commentary. There are plenty of jokes in *Joseph Andrews,* and plenty of things to make us laugh that are not exactly jokes, but the prominence of the joke teller can be off-putting. Although the narrator is playful, some readers find him a nuisance because he is intrusive, but his role is crucial to Fielding's conception of the novel in 1742. One effect of the novel's humor is to make the narrator as conspicuous as possible, and to bring the narrator and the reader closer together, which ultimately accords with the satiric thrust of *Joseph Andrews.*

In this chapter I want to explore some of the various ways in which Fielding seeks to make his readers laugh, and what the implications of that laughter might be. Rather than qualify everything I may say about Fielding's humor, I shall refer to various things as funny, but

I do not assume that everyone necessarily finds them funny. Writing or talking about humor is never easy, because the subject is nearly always funnier than the discussion of it. I warn my readers now that this is a chapter without a joke in it.

It is very hard to say what anyone finds funny, and even harder to say why some things make us laugh. With due wariness, then, I ask: What sort of thing did Fielding find funny? Incongruity, slapstick, word play, extremes. There is a certain amount of Fielding in the absurdity of Monty Python: the seemingly endless qualifying phrases, the figures of authority like judges who are stupid or corrupt, who ridicule themselves and so become figures of fun, and so on. A different kind of answer to my question would involve the ideas that Fielding laughed at: women who like a drink, or who cannot resist the temptation to look at themselves in a mirror, a little weak man who fancies that he is a big, strong one, a woman who is repellent in appearance thinking she is fantastically attractive. These are accessible enough to us today, but there are occasional obstacles to our enjoyment of Fielding's humor. In some places Fielding inserts allusions, many of them unquestionably intended to be funny, to people whom we now know only through an editor's explanatory notes. For instance, when we discover that Parson Adams has been fast asleep while Joseph is praising John Kyrle and Ralph Allen, and that Adams would have slept even if Orator Henley had been before him, we do lose some of the significance that these allusions to living people had for readers in 1742. There is not much we can do about that loss except to rely on a scholarly editor's recovery of the relevant information. But although we lose something here, and although most readers do not know the real people on whom several characters in *Joseph Andrews* are modeled, the humor of this novel does not depend in the main on local or topical allusions.

Joseph Andrews is nevertheless a novel that reflects its time (as all novels do) and so some of Fielding's humor probably will not strike modern readers as funny at all, but it can act as a guide to eighteenth-century social conventions. I do not find anything funny about Lady Booby's "refreshing her Spirits with a small Cordial which she kept in her Closet [a small private room]" (44; 1, 9), but the point is that she keeps a secret stash of liquor, which would probably have amused Fielding's contemporaries because ladies in high society were not politely thought to do such things. Of course in reality they did, but the genteel fiction was maintained that they did not. Rather than explain every such tiny example of humorous intent, I am concerned in this chapter with Fielding's methods and the implications of what he chooses as vehicles for his humor. So I am looking less at a woman who likes a drink and more at Fielding's way of trying to make such a woman seem funny to his readers, and the consequences to which our attention might be drawn. This way, I can also avoid the impossible task of being psychologist to Fielding.

Fielding's simplest visual and physical humor occurs in several scenes, especially early in the narrative, that typify the jokey tone of the novel as a whole. Apart from the two rather cruel caricatures—Slipslop with her bovine breasts and Mrs. Tow-wouse with her pinched face—Fielding's style does not depend much on visual description, but it does make demands on our visual imagination. In this example, Lady Booby tells Mrs. Slipslop to fire Joseph:

> Mrs. *Slipslop* went out, and the Lady had scarce taken two turns before she fell to knocking and ringing with great Violence. *Slipslop*, who did not travel post-haste, soon returned, and was countermanded as to *Joseph*, but ordered to send *Betty* about her Business without delay [that is, fire her]. She went out a second time with much greater alacrity than before; when the Lady began immediately to accuse herself of Want of Resolution, and to apprehend the Return of her Affection with its pernicious Consequences: she therefore applied herself again to the Bell, and resummoned Mrs. *Slipslop* into her Presence; who again returned, and was told by her Mistress, that she had consider'd better of the Matter, and was absolutely resolved to turn away *Joseph*. (35–36; 1, 7)

This seesawing continues, as Slipslop leaves a third time, Lady Booby calls her back again, sends her out, and would call her back yet again, "but could not prevail with herself" (36; 1, 7). It is easy to imagine a scene like this working well in a theater, where with good timing from the actresses, the humor would be even more conspicuously based on Lady Booby's fluctuating passion at odds with her reason. The continual exits and entrances of Mrs. Slipslop are really not funny, but Lady Booby's wild extremes are. There is nothing very complex about Lady Booby's lust for Joseph, here or anywhere else in the novel, nor is she in truth the "Heroine." Since she turns out to have a rather minor role in the narrative, this scene cannot easily be taken as a great revelation of character, nor anything else of such significance. Fielding seems to have designed his humor here with no other end in view than to raise a laugh for its own sake. Yet because this scene occurs early in the novel, it helps to set the tone, or the mood, of the narrative. One other side effect of the scene is that it heightens the contrast between the ferocious lust of the women (Mrs. Slipslop has just been compared to "a hungry Tygress" preparing to sink her claws into Joseph) and Joseph's rather ludicrously decorous (and naive) care for his chastity.

The scenes involving one accident or another befalling Parson Adams are similarly physical, and simple in their humor, but they too are not without their significance. Adams wades through a pond, and of course gets soaked in the process, only to discover that there was a way he could have walked around the water (96; 2, 2); or, "*Adams's* Foot slipping, he instantly disappeared, which greatly frighted both *Joseph* and *Fanny*; indeed, if the Light had permitted them to see it, they would scarce have refrained laughing to see the Parson rolling down the Hill, which he did from top to bottom, without receiving any harm" (194; 3, 2). Along with the sequence of "*several curious Night-Adventures*" (330; 4, 14), in which everyone contrives to get into someone else's bed, these are typical instances of a brand of humor that again helps to establish and maintain the tone of the narrative. Characters are always tumbling over, getting messy, spilling things, falling off horses, and so forth; instead of a custard pie, we have a hog's pudding, but this very visual humor is basic slapstick of a kind that Fielding had exploited in his years as a playwright and that is most familiar to us now from the action of a silent movie.

Even slapstick can have some more substantial point to make.

The "roasting" scene (244–51; 3, 7) consists of one practical joke after another in slapstick mode, but at least it reveals something—albeit not very much—about the mentality of a brainless forty-year-old bachelor who enjoys causing other people discomfort. More important perhaps, this scene reveals the good nature of Adams, who is the butt of humiliating and brutish humor, and although "enraged," does no more than walk out of the house without retaliating (251; 3, 7). The coarse slapstick of this scene therefore adds to our knowledge of the character of the parson, and stresses the value and attractiveness of good nature, one of Fielding's main themes in the novel.

In contrast with the physical, much of Fielding's humor is verbal. The sort of humor I have in mind is typified by his addresses to love and vanity, his piling up of example after example (laying it on thick), his calculated understatements, mockery of epic language, long sequences of qualifications, and parody. I will deal here with two or three examples. The address to vanity, which carries a thoroughly serious point too—that vanity is a dangerous and widespread human trait—is humorous because it is so marvelously exaggerated. Here Fielding uses the tones and rhythms of an epic poet's invocation of his muse:

> O Vanity! How little is thy Force acknowledged, or thy Operations discerned? How wantonly dost thou deceive Mankind under different Disguises? . . . The greatest Villanies are daily practised to please thee: nor is the meanest Thief below, or the greatest Hero above thy notice. Thy Embraces are often the sole Aim and sole Reward of the private Robbery, and the plundered Province. . . . All our Passions are thy Slaves. Avarice itself is often no more than thy Hand-maid, and even Lust thy Pimp. The Bully Fear like a Coward, flies before thee, and Joy and Grief hide their Heads in thy Presence. (69; 1, 15)

If "this sarcastical Panegyrick" (70; 1, 15) seems less funny out of context, that is as it should be, because this address to vanity is expressed in deliberately contrasting language: part of the humor of interpolations like this one comes from the jolt as we move from the fairly casual, relaxed tone of the narrative to this highly formal mode. Fielding gives us a typical reminder of the difference in tone by adding anticlimactically that this address was "introduced . . . for no other Purpose than to lengthen out a short Chapter" (70; 1, 15). That contrast is significant, for a reason that will become apparent in a moment.

It is characteristic of Fielding's verbal wit to inflate his language in other contexts as well. In the messiest battle scene, Adams punches the innkeeper on the nose, and the innkeeper punches him back: "*Adams* dealt him so sound a Compliment over his Face with his Fist, that the Blood immediately gushed out of his Nose in a Stream. The Host being unwilling to be outdone in Courtesy, especially by a Person of *Adams's* Figure, returned the Favour with so much Gratitude, that the Parson's Nostrils likewise began to look a little redder than usual" (119; 2, 5). Likewise, when the hostess throws her pan of pig's blood at Adams, the blood does not just splash onto his face, it "first saluted his Countenance, and trickled thence in so large a current down his Beard, and over his Garments, that a more horrible Spectacle was hardly to be seen or even imagined" (120; 2, 5). When the language is similarly inflated in the scene where Adams and Joseph do battle with a pack of hunting dogs, Fielding has his full mock-epic apparatus at work, and there he reminds us that because the battle is now over, "we shall therefore proceed in our ordinary Style with the Continuation of this History" (242; 3, 6).

The other kinds of verbal humor that I mentioned have the same tendency toward exaggeration. Even the understatements are extreme. For instance, the extreme grotesquerie of Slipslop's ghastly appearance is coupled with the understatement that "She was not at this time remarkably handsome" (32; 1, 6). Likewise, the chambermaid Betty avoids "those other ill Effects, which prudent young Women very justly apprehend from too absolute an Indulgence to the pressing Endearments of their Lovers" (87; 1, 18). She is unfaithful to her lover, John, but Fielding phrases it much more delicately and tentatively than that: "This latter, perhaps, was a little owing to her not being entirely constant to *John*, with whom she permitted *Tom Whipwell* the

Stage-Coachman, and now and then a handsome young Traveller, to share her Favours" (87; 1, 18). The casual insertion of "and now and then a handsome young Traveller" is a wonderfully understated way of saying that she sleeps with anyone she fancies, and so it contrasts ironically with the phrase that ranges Betty among "prudent young Women." But probably the best example of Fielding's exaggerated language is this:

> You have heard, Reader, Poets talk of the *Statue of Surprize;* you have heard likewise, or else you have heard very little, how Surprize made one of the Sons of *Croesus* speak tho' he was dumb. You have seen the Faces, in the Eighteen-penny Gallery [of a theater], when, through the Trap-Door, to soft or no Musick, Mr. *Bridgewater,* Mr. *William Mills* [both actors], or some other of ghostly Appearance, hath ascended with a Face all pale with Powder, and a Shirt all Bloody with Ribbons; but from none of these, nor from *Phidias,* or *Praxiteles,* if they should return to Life—no, not from the inimitable Pencil of my Friend *Hogarth,* could you receive such an Idea of Surprize, as would have entered in at your Eyes, had they beheld the Lady *Booby,* when those last Words issued from the Lips of *Joseph.*—Your Virtue! (said the Lady recovering after a Silence of two Minutes) I shall never survive it. Your Virtue! (40–41; 1, 8)

What does such comic exaggeration achieve? Apart from being funny in its own right (most readers I know do laugh at this), this elaborate insertion, like the other examples of verbal extremes, establishes a distinctive narrative voice. This is all evidence of a controller, a narrator who has power over the words, someone who offers interpretation and commentary, someone who will delay the punch line until he sees fit.

One of this narrator's richest humorous veins is the manipulation, use, and abuse of language. Obviously, Fielding thought that people who got their words wrong were pretty funny: Colley Cibber, for instance, "who lived the Life he hath recorded, and is by many thought to have lived such a Life only in order to write it" (18; 1, 1). There are several jabs at Cibber's notably incorrect English and his eccentric phrasing (e.g., 273; 3, 12). Mrs. Slipslop's "hard words," which nobody understands, are a more obvious source of fun, if somewhat labored fun. Richard Brinsley Sheridan invented Mrs. Malaprop and gave her name to the English language in 1775, but Fielding had actually anticipated that most celebrated of linguistic torturers in 1742. Mrs. Slipslop gets numerous words muddled: "confidous" when she means "confident," "result" for "repulse," "refer" for "prefer," and so on. But sometimes her meaning is less obvious:

> Sure nothing can be a more simple *Contract* in a Woman, than to place her Affections on a Boy. If I had ever thought it would have been my Fate, I should have wished to die a thousand Deaths rather than live to see that Day. If we like a Man, the lightest Hint *sophisticates*. Whereas a Boy *proposes* upon us to break through all the *Regulations* of Modesty, before we can make any *Oppression* on him. (33; 1, 6)

Since her "hard words" are homonyms, "oppression" for "impression" is appropriate, but of course it is appropriate in another way, because she would "oppress" Joseph if given the chance. And in this society, modesty does indeed have regulations. If anything is funny about Slipslop's language, it is the ironic implication, I think, rather than the actual confusion of words, which is a joke that does not stand up to very much repetition. Behind Mrs. Slipslop's peculiar language is Mrs. Slipslop herself, trying to sound sophisticated by imitating the polysyllabic speech of her "superiors," but the fact remains that she makes a fool of herself. Her speech is paralleled by her sticking her nose in the air and pretending not to know Fanny (155; 2, 12). There again "that high Woman" Slipslop is imitating her "superiors," and the narrator at once proceeds to explain something about perceived social status. Slipslop's language is a sign of her attempt to rise above herself, and so if it makes us laugh at all, it may be at her endeavor to be taken for someone "better" than she really is.

A closely related aspect of language and its abuse occurs elsewhere in *Joseph Andrews*. Doctors and lawyers speak in professional jargon, which, of course, no one else understands. Fielding certainly preferred people to speak in plain English. One of his own standard ways of drawing attention to plain English was to do something like this:

> Now the Rake *Hesperus* had called for his Breeches, and having well rubbed his drowsy Eyes, prepared to dress himself for all Night; by whose Example his Brother Rakes on Earth likewise leave those Beds, in which they had slept away the Day. Now *Thetis* the good Housewife began to put on the Pot in order to regale the good Man *Phoebus,* after his daily Labours were over. In vulgar Language, it was in the Evening when *Joseph* attended his Lady's Orders. (37–38; 1, 8)

The incongruity of the mock-epic (*"some very fine Writing,"* announces the chapter heading) is clear even without such additions as "in a word" or "in vulgar Language." Many of the ridiculous characters speak in pompous English and sound silly when plain language would be effective and comprehensible. This probably does not mean that Fielding was like those people who constantly write letters to the news programs on National Public Radio to complain that a reporter mispronounces a word or misuses a phrase. Fielding was not some crank with an obsession about "correct" English, but he may have seen something faintly sinister in the misuse of language. A typical Fielding doctor declares in ringing tones: "The Contusion on his Head has *perforated* the *internal Membrane* of the *Occiput,* and *divellicated* that *radical* small *minute* invisible *Nerve,* which *coheres* to the *Pericranium;* and this was attended with a Fever at first *symptomatick,* then *pneumatick,* and he is at length *grown deliruus,* or delirious, as the Vulgar express it" (63; 1, 14). This specialized vocabulary might well make sense to a doctor, and actually it makes sense to the intelligent reader too—whatever "divellicated" may mean—because this character is not really saying anything very complicated, but only trying to sound impressive to his audience. This self-important doctor, we know, is the one who goes back to bed, even though he is already half dressed, because he discovers that the patient he should treat is not rich. The key to Fielding's humor is the last sentence: the man who distinguishes between "deliruus" and "delirious" evidently places himself above "the Vulgar," just as the narrator does with his talk of Phoebus and Thetis—but of course the narrator is being ironic. The effect of the doctor's pointless pomposity is therefore similar to that of Mrs. Slipslop's: he wants to be thought superior. Even Mrs. Slipslop's muddled speech could, I suppose, be called a specialized vocabulary. Doctors, lawyers, academics, and, in more recent times, economists have developed specialized vocabularies, but there is more to Fielding's satire of such people than identifying the silly pomposity with which they use their jargon. Fielding recognized also that lawyers and doctors especially had invented a complicated language to conceal simple matters, knowing that ordinary people would not understand them. They could then charge exorbitant fees for interpreting the language or, as Gulliver says,

> this Society [i.e., of lawyers] hath a peculiar Cant and Jargon of their own, that no other Mortal can understand, and wherein all their Laws are written, which they take special Care to multiply; whereby they have wholly confounded the very Essence of Truth and Falsehood, of Right and Wrong; so that it will take Thirty Years to decide whether the Field, left me by my Ancestors for six Generations, belong to me, or to a Stranger three Hundred Miles off.[30]

Gulliver has already mentioned that lawyers prove "by Words multiplied for the Purpose, that *White* is *Black,* and *Black* is *White,* according as they are paid."[31] Some recognition of this manipulation of language for profit lies behind Fielding's humor at the expense of such professional men, not any deep-seated conservatism about "correct" English.

I have suggested that apart from the very simplest joking, Fielding's humor leads to rather more serious issues. It is not the amusing quirk of someone's speech that matters, but what that quirk suggests—pomposity, self-importance, ambition, greed—not intrinsically funny things at all. Ultimately, this means that Fielding's humor is a vehicle for satire. One mode that any satirist is likely to use is irony, and there is plenty of that in Fielding's humorous tone, too. I should say that irony is the characteristic tone of the novel's narrator, whether or not there is satiric intent, but for the moment I restrict myself to irony for humorous effect. A typical example occurs at the moment when we learn that Adams has successfully borrowed a guinea, "for so good was the Credit of Mr. *Adams,* that even Mr. *Peter* the Lady *Booby's* Steward, would have lent him a Guinea with very little Security" (94; 2, 2). The main point of the remark, and of the paragraph as a whole, is that Adams is trustworthy. The ironic point, that Peter Pounce would nonetheless demand security, is slipped in. Much of the humorous irony of the novel functions in this way, almost like an aside in a play.

A further example would be Peter Pounce again, "a very gallant Person, [who] loved a pretty Girl better than any thing, besides his own Money, or the Money of other People" (269; 3, 12). One effect of this kind of irony is that it establishes (or is designed to establish) a kind of agreement between narrator and reader. If readers do agree with the narrator's condemnation of minor characters like Peter Pounce, they will more probably share his moral views on the big issues. The ironies concerning Peter Pounce here confirm what we already know about him, for the narrator has been quite explicit as his irony shades into sarcasm about this usurer, "who, on urgent Occasions, used to advance the Servants their Wages: not before they were due, but before they were payable; that is, perhaps, half a Year after they were due, and this at the moderate *Premiums* of fifty *per Cent.* or a little more; by which charitable Methods, together with lending Money to other People, and even to his own Master and Mistress, the honest Man had, from nothing, in a few Years amassed a small Sum of twenty thousand Pounds or thereabouts" (47; 1, 10). So if we condemn (as it were) the pathological cupidity of a steward holding poor servants' wages for six months and then in effect withholding more than half the money, we are being led to do so by the very obviously ironic tones of the narrator. In Fielding's technique, readers need that narrator, for satire needs a satirist. Mockery is not funny unless we share a point of view with the mocker. As several critics have pointed out, if we laugh as we read *Joseph Andrews*, our laughter is continuous with the narrator's. If we share his point of view, we agree that Peter Pounce is not honest at all.

To call a man as mean and scheming as Peter Pounce "honest" is plainly incongruous, just as Mrs. Slipslop's putting on airs is incongruous, or, to take an example from the preface, "a dirty Fellow" who "descend[s] from his Coach and Six, or bolt[s] from his Chair with his Hat under his Arm" (9; preface) would be incongruous. Mrs. Slipslop and the dirty fellow are examples of inappropriate behavior. Someone who rides in a coach and six—the eighteenth century's equivalent of a Rolls Royce—is expected to be clean and well dressed, apparently. And when you step out of a chair (equivalent to a taxicab, more or less), you are expected to put your hat on and walk away. What is inappropriate or incongruous is someone trying to be what he is not. That is Mrs. Slipslop's problem, too, as she imitates Lady Booby without belonging to Lady Booby's social class. On a much more serious level, Peter Pounce *seems* to be what he is not: he seems to be honest. If we find any of these characteristics ridiculous, as Fielding's preface tells us we probably will, then we are laughing at hypocrisy in varying degrees of intensity.

6

Ancestry, Birth, Class

There is a moment in Richardson's *Clarissa* when Lovelace, who is aristocratic, expresses nothing but scorn for a pair of petty bourgeois shopkeepers who equip their shop with a seat under "an arched kind of canopy carved work, which these proud traders, emulating the royal niche-fillers, often give themselves, while a joint-stool perhaps serves those by whom they get their bread: such is the dignity of trade in this mercantile nation!"[32] We can glimpse several things here, compressed into this one brief observation. An aristocrat has contempt for the dignity that tradesmen award themselves. The nation is mercantile. Traders are proud. Traders imitate upper class people ("royal niche-fillers"). Traders have inappropriate taste: they opt for something fancy, while the people to whom they sell their goods are quite satisfied with something simple (a joint stool). This small example also indicates that traditional class distinctions were becoming a bit blurred in the eighteenth century. I mentioned earlier that the middle class was growing in numbers and wealth, and therefore power, at an unprecedented rate. The distinction between the middle class and the classes above them—gentry, aristocracy—began to seem less precise once tradesmen began to behave like their "betters."

In the real world as in Richardson's fictional world, it seems that middle-class people did assert their dignity and importance, as people often do when they suddenly gain money, power, or fame. It is risky to talk in general terms of middle-class mentality, values, and so on, but it appears anyway that British middle-class people as a whole also created the impression—whether they meant to or not—that they held a monopoly on decency, morality, sobriety, endeavor, and enterprise. Britain's middle-class population in Fielding's time was mostly Protestant, and many of them were Puritan, and so they tended to articulate such concepts as the work ethic, and sometimes their views on various social matters were just ordinary Puritan points of view but sounded like strident dissatisfaction with someone else. In other words, to people such as Lovelace who did not like them, the middle class sounded holier-than-thou, arrogant, priggish, and self-important.

Fielding's novels take cognizance of this middle-class expansion, and of the articulation of middle-class attitudes, but his novels all tend to confirm the status quo, that is, to conserve class hierarchy the way it is. People who oppose Marxist analysis often deny that class consciousness is a motivating factor in people's lives, but whatever the truth of such propositions may be, *Joseph Andrews* is a very class-conscious novel. Class and attitudes associated with class account for the behavior of several characters. As I have already suggested, class is defined (in British culture) in terms of birth, and thus of ancestry as well. The typical plot of a romance revolves around birth and ancestry: it is based on the revelation of the true circumstances of the hero's birth, which usually turns out to be socially higher, or more respectable, than everyone had thought. The plot of *Joseph Andrews* follows this pattern, with Joseph turning out to be the son of a gentleman (though Adams had hoped the lost son might be "some Great Man, or Duke" [225; 3, 4]). Such a plot is not necessarily a confirmation of any particular attitude about class, nor necessarily a commentary on it. My point is that such a plot is built around class, almost to the point of taking it for granted, and so would be impossible without a ready-made set of definitions, assumptions, and attitudes about class.

In romances that use this conventional arrangement of plot,

heroes are usually elevated (at the end) socially and materially: happiness, financial benefits, at any rate rewards of some kind are showered on men (or occasionally, women) who were, it turns out, born in a higher class. This association of desirable things with high class actually entrenches the idea that there are class distinctions, that high class is itself desirable, and that the lower down you are on the social scale the more likely you are to be miserable, poor, and downtrodden. Whether or not that is true, fiction of this kind confirms class hierarchy and attaches values to it. Even the standard vocabulary is revealing, the key words being quality, birth, fortune, and betters. Without for one moment suggesting anything demeaning about Fanny, Adams praises her virtue by wishing "that all her Betters were as good" as she (158; 2, 13). Similarly, Betty roars at Mrs. Tow-wouse for calling her a bitch, "'and if I have been no better than I should be,' cries she sobbing, 'that's no Reason you should call me out of my Name; my Be—Betters are wo—worse than me'" (85; 1, 17). This was the common vocabulary of the day: people born in more privileged circumstances were the "betters" of a Betty or a Fanny. There are many other similar instances of language that is really loaded with implications that high-class people are somehow superior. One important aspect of Fielding's satire is to show that they are not. Another is to show that the rising middle class is no better.

When Wilson tells his story, he includes numerous passing comments on matters of class and concomitant behavior. He speaks, for example, of the unpleasant conduct of those people "whose Birth and Fortunes place them just without [i.e., outside] the polite Circles; I mean the lower Class of the Gentry, and the higher of the mercantile World" (217–18; 3, 3). He is talking of people precisely at the borderline, where the upper middle class is striving to climb to the same social level as the gentry, precisely where there was that blurring of an old distinction I mentioned at the beginning of this chapter. Neither Wilson nor Fielding seems too worried about the distinction. What troubles Wilson is the way these people conduct themselves: they "are in reality the worst bred part of Mankind" (218; 3, 3). That is the point: these people have no manners, no compassion, and they take pleasure in causing others discomfort. But, in the course of Wilson's story, this is a minor point, because the main business of the story is to show that it is possible for good sense to triumph over the worldliness and silliness, and over the hypocrisy of course, of fashionable society (and "fashionable," Fielding will tell us later, means "high").

Wilson is one of many figures in this novel who frame what they say and think in terms of class, rank, or hierarchy. Lady Booby does it, when she prompts Slipslop to parrot her. Slipslop always says whatever she thinks is the answer Lady Booby wants to hear, but toward the end of the novel she is none too confident of getting her answer right. But right on cue Slipslop damns Fanny, "concluding with the Observation that there was always something in those low-life Creatures which must eternally distinguish them from their Betters" (295; 4, 6). In the course of the comic conversation that follows, Lady Booby maintains the transparent pretense that she is not interested (sexually) in Joseph, but the constant tenor of what she says, and what Slipslop echoes, is based on class distinction. What this means is that Lady Booby is justifying her passion for a footman by saying that he behaves really like a gentleman. He is "so genteel that a Prince might without a Blush acknowledge him for a Son," and as she enumerates his virtues (real ones), she keeps coming back to matters of rank:

> And then for his Virtues; such Piety to his Parents, such tender Affection to his Sister, such Integrity in his Friendship, such Bravery, such Goodness, that *if he had been born a Gentleman, his Wife would have possest the most invaluable Blessing.* . . . Is he not more worthy of Affection than a dirty Country Clown, tho' born of a Family as old as the Flood, or an idle worthless Rake, or a little puisny [puny] Beau of Quality? And yet these we must condemn ourselves to, in order to avoid the Censure of the World; to shun the Contempt of others, we must ally ourselves to those we despise; *we must prefer Birth, Title and Fortune to real Merit.* It is a Tyranny of Custom, a Tyranny we must comply with: For we People of Fashion are the Slaves of Custom. (296; 4, 6; my italics)

These words nicely express Lady Booby's dilemma: custom determines fashion, and fashion prevents an upper class lady from acknowledging her sexual passion for a man of a lower class, even though she recognizes and genuinely values Joseph's good qualities. Since Lady Booby's lust for Joseph is the focus of everything we know about her in the novel, it is her defining characteristic, and she expresses it in terms of birth and quality, or class. It is a theme she cannot leave alone (327–28; 4, 13).

This habit of thinking in terms of class is not restricted only to the Lady Boobys of the world: the narrator does the same. In keeping with one custom of romance, and "in conformity to the exact Rules of Biography" (21; 1, 2), Fielding's second chapter introduces the subject of Joseph's "Birth, Parentage, Education, and great Endowments, with a Word or two concerning Ancestors" (20; 1, 2, chapter heading). Joseph's great endowments are his beautiful voice, his good looks, and a rather dubious priapic tendency. Before getting to those attributes Fielding makes fun of the current novelistic practice of providing a kind of family history of the protagonist:

> Mr. *Joseph Andrews,* the Hero of our ensuing History, was esteemed to be the only Son of Gaffar and Gammer *Andrews,* and Brother to the illustrious *Pamela,* whose Virtue is at present so famous. As to his Ancestors, we have searched with great Diligence, but little Success: being unable to trace them farther than his Great Grandfather, who, as an elderly Person in the Parish remembers to have heard his Father say, was an excellent Cudgel-player. Whether he had any Ancestors before this, we must leave to the Opinion of our curious Reader, finding nothing of sufficient Certainty to relie on. (20; 1, 2)

We have here a parody of the oral history method of researching one's ancestors. Joseph might have been the grandson of a man who could wield a cudgel, but it is hardly vital information and it is barely relevant to anything. But when the narrator leaves it up to us to determine *whether* Joseph had any earlier ancestors, we know he has to be joking.

There is also a serious note beneath the joke. Joseph is the son of Gaffar and Gammer Andrews. Nowadays, the boss in the workplace might be called "the gaffer" (the usual spelling) but only among members of the working class—not among white-collar workers. As Dr. Johnson defined it in 1755, gaffer was "a word of respect now obsolete, or applied only in contempt to a mean person." "Gammer" is the corresponding female equivalent. There is therefore something slightly self-conscious about calling Joseph the son of Gaffar and Gammer Andrews, and not, let us say, of Mr. and Mrs. or John and Mary Andrews (or some such names). "Gaffar" and "Gammer" place them precisely as "mean persons," as members of the lowest social class. There is much more in *Joseph Andrews* to reinforce this social placing. Anyway, Joseph is their son, and brother of the famously virtuous Pamela. Fielding (of course) could have made Joseph anybody's brother, or omitted siblings altogether, but he made him Pamela's brother, and therefore reminded readers that Richardson's Pamela is the daughter of two "mean persons." All in all, this is Fielding's tiny, sly reminder that in Richardson's novel Pamela is of low class, and that she marries a squire, who is of a much higher class; it is a way of reminding readers that there is a class basis for Richardson's fiction. In fact, the snobbery and self-importance that accompanied that basis are the things that Fielding disliked most about *Pamela*. Students sometimes ask me if I think Fielding would consciously have thought all this through, and in these terms, to which the answer must be yes, because when he has Mr. Booby and Pamela, near the end, trying to persuade Joseph not to marry Fanny, they argue that Fanny is "beneath" them. When Joseph protests that Fanny is Pamela's equal, " 'She was my Equal,' answered *Pamela*, 'but I am no longer *Pamela Andrews*, I am now this Gentleman's Lady, and as such am above her'" (302; 4, 7). As in *Shamela*, so now in *Joseph Andrews*, Fielding is not expressing discontent with the idea that a servant can marry a gentleman, but he is satirizing the sudden transformation into snobbery that he thought Richardson's *Pamela* seemed to sanction. Fielding detested snobbery in anyone, but especially in people who had nothing to be snobbish about.

Book 1, chapter 2, is one small example of how class gives a slant to Fielding's narrative. It confirms the preoccupation with birth and rank as a basis on which people deal with one another. Again and again, people in this novel judge other people by appearance. They do so in real life, too. In this novel, though, they judge other people's class by appearance. For example, the men who are sent to capture Fanny say that "notwithstanding her Disguise, her Air, which she could not conceal, sufficiently discovered her Birth to be infinitely superior" to those of Joseph and Adams (257; 3, 9). There are many more such examples in *Joseph Andrews,* with a greater concentration of this and other aspects of class toward the end of the novel, when Pamela, Lady Booby, and Mr. Booby are trying to maneuver Fanny out of the way. The fact is that Lady Booby has a carnal motive for getting rid of Fanny—so that she can get her hands (literally) on Joseph. Lady Booby's son and his wife, Pamela, have no such motive, but go along with her for reasons that are mostly snobbish (Lady Booby's appeal to her son is based entirely on class snobbery [301; 4, 7]). They all imagine that if they appeal to the concept of class by saying that Fanny is too "low" for such a socially exalted family, they will convince Joseph to abandon Fanny. (It never occurs to them that Pamela was once just as "low" herself.) They think they have a strong case, but they do not. Joseph rejects their arguments because he values Fanny's virtues (which they scorn and dismiss) above any considerations of her birth, and puts love above social rank. We know that Joseph is *extremely* virtuous, to the point of being comically absurd, so we know that he is unusual. It should follow, then, that his is the unusual line of defense against their arguments, and that their arguments would represent the majority view, and that they are "normal." If that is so, we would deduce that arguments based on class appeal usually do succeed. But their attitudes to class are thus being exposed as snobbish and unfeeling, and as such they are close to the heart of Fielding's use of class in this novel.

One of the striking features of *Joseph Andrews* is just how much emphasis there is on matters of ancestry and birth, hierarchy and rank. In that second chapter, Fielding's narrator first dismisses the question of ancestors, then at once returns to it, declaring that someone of obscure birth "might be related to some Persons of very great Figure at present" (21; 1, 2); but his main point, really, is that if we are not distracted by considerations of class, we can and should look at some-one's virtues. It is not equality or democracy that matters for Fielding, but a recognition that people can have good moral qualities whoever their parents are, and those qualities, not their ancestors, are what make them admirable people.

Individual characters, too, are preoccupied with rank, even those who do most to undermine it. One such character is Joseph himself. Not only does he behave deferentially toward Lady Booby (granted, it is his job to do so), but he also reprimands a surly innkeeper for arguing with Adams: Joseph bids him "know how to behave himself to his Betters" (119; 2, 5). The innkeeper is already predisposed to treat Joseph and Adams with scorn or neglect, for "observing his Wife on her Knees to a Footman [tending Joseph's wounded leg, he] cried out, without considering the Circumstances, 'What a Pox is the Woman about? why don't you mind the Company in the Coach?'" (119; 2, 5). Now even if Joseph is thinking of Adams's qualities as a good man, his words suggest that Adams is of a higher class than the innkeeper. Not surprisingly, the innkeeper, who prefers upper class coach passengers to a mere footman about whom he cares not a jot, certainly takes Joseph's words as a slur, and the messy battle begins.

The pattern established in book 1 is repeated, with variations, throughout the novel, such as when Adams is so dirty and messy that Peter Pounce, though nearly laughing, will not "accept his Homage in that Pickle" (270; 3, 12). Homage indeed! This might remind us that Sir Thomas and Lady Booby regard Adams as a "mere" domestic servant (25; 1, 3). Class is everywhere, in everyday situations, and as in these examples it is mingled with pride or haughtiness. In one typical instance, class is the major point of a scene. Miss Grave-airs causes delay and annoyance to fellow passengers because of her class prejudices:

> she would not admit a Footman into the Coach. . . . A young Lady, who was, as it seems, an Earl's Grand Daughter, begged it with almost Tears in her Eyes [true nobility]; Mr. *Adams* prayed [i.e., asked politely], and Mrs. *Slipslop* scolded, but all to no purpose.

> She said, "she would not demean herself to ride with a Footman:
> that there were Waggons on the Road: that if the Master of the
> Coach desired it, she would pay for two Places: but would suffer
> no such Fellow to come in." (123; 2, 5)

One might observe at this point that it occurs to none of them to
overrule Miss Grave-airs. No one uses force, no one brushes her or
her objections aside: instead, they defer to her prejudice. What follows
is an argument between her and Mrs. Slipslop, which has an added
comic edge because it is a furious verbal row about snobbery con-
ducted by two snobs. That neither woman has the least reason to be
snobbish also emerges. We know it already of Slipslop, and we learn
it in a few sentences about Miss Grave-airs, whose father, says the
coachman, "was no better born than myself" (124; 2, 5). Ah! Adams
"thought *she was some such Trollop*" (124; 2, 5). Slipslop is far from
pleased to hear this news because it might eventually damage her own
"Interest with her Mistress," and all the passengers proceed in due
course to discuss "the Character of Miss *Grave-airs*." They also discuss, with relish, her status as a gentlewoman and her corresponding
moral behavior: they discuss her class.

In the scene with Miss Grave-airs, Mrs. Slipslop plays a somewhat ambivalent role, which is consistent with her function in the
novel as a mirror to Lady Booby. Slipslop is ultimately a personification of hypocrisy and snobbery. Her absurd behavior, such as her pretense that she does not know Fanny, is not just a pose for posing's
sake, it is a pose meant to suggest her own higher social rank. That
much we can deduce from a single adjective. Fanny curtsies to Slipslop, "but that high Woman would not return her Curt'sies; but cast-
ing her Eyes another way, immediately withdrew into another Room,
muttering as she went, she wondered *who the Creature was*" (155; 2,
12). This behavior is explained in the next chapter, which distinguishes between "high" and "low" people. There we learn that Slipslop's behavior was entirely normal, "and indeed, had she done
otherwise, she must have descended below herself, and would have
been very justly liable to Censure" (156; 2, 13). By high and low Field-

ing says he means fashionable and not fashionable, but as his disquisition continues it becomes clear that he is describing a social hierarchy in which all people regard themselves as above *someone,* whom they can accordingly treat with contempt. The behavior of this hierarchical society is in "the common Road" (156; 2, 13).

Time after time, *Joseph Andrews* shows characters placing a higher value on class than on moral qualities. Even Joseph himself, in asserting his virtue to Lady Booby, reveals that he would not transgress class boundaries: "'*Ladies! Madam,*' said *Joseph,* '*I am sure I never had the Impudence to think of any that deserve that Name*'" (29; 1, 5); it would, he thinks, be presumption on the part of a lowly footman to make an amorous overture to a *lady.* And Joseph is, as C. J. Rawson has noticed, something of a parody of a gentleman rather than a real gentleman. It is really a distinction between nature and nurture, for Joseph is born a real gentleman (without knowing it) but does not quite manage to carry himself like one: he has "the most perfect Neatness in his Dress, and an Air, which to those who have not seen many Noblemen, would give an Idea of Nobility" (38–39; 1, 8). But those who *have* seen many noblemen would, presumably, not be deceived by such an appearance.[33]

Whether he is or is not genuinely noble in his manner, Joseph is unaffected, honest, and candid. Not so Lady Booby, Mrs. Slipslop, and a host of others. The novel is filled with characters who go to extraordinary lengths to avoid being thought to be of a lower class than the one they belong to. In a parallel formation, many of them want to be thought to belong to a higher class. It is a running theme of book 1, especially in the scenes at Mrs. Tow-wouse's inn and in those on the road leading there, that people try very hard to avoid being associated with the low, or the poor, or the wretched, or the criminal, all of which categories get muddled. These are the scenes involving Joseph's being attacked, stripped, beaten, robbed, and abandoned, then picked up and transported in a passing stagecoach to an inn, where he recovers. Nobody in the coach wants to pick him up at all, nor lend him a coat, until the humane postilion damns them all for their unfeeling lack of charity. As I suggested earlier, the stagecoach scene reveals the hypocrisy of the passengers more than anything: they all look out for themselves and lie to avoid sharing anything they have with them. Their behavior is paralleled by that of the doctor, who goes to the trouble of undressing and returning to his bed when he finds out that his patient is only "a poor foot Passenger" (55; 1, 12), and by that of Mrs. Tow-wouse, who is suddenly and irrationally prompted to fear an invasion by "scabby Rascals" and "poor Wretches" (56; 1, 12).

There is more of this sort, all of it fairly obvious, as Mrs. Tow-wouse chides her pusillanimous husband for welcoming a mob of fellows because they were "Beggars and Thieves," which in fact they are not (65; 1, 14). Parallel to the doctor, the local magistrate is more interested in whether or not Adams is a gentleman than he is in innocence or guilt (149; 2, 11). He acquits gentlemen but convicts "low fellows." It would be easy to multiply examples, but there is no need. To take Mrs. Tow-wouse as the main example from the sequence in which she appears, what emerges is not just her nastiness, her violent temper, and her grating voice. Basically snobbish, she puts on airs, just like Mrs. Slipslop in another context, which I have discussed earlier. Both women are desperate to be thought to belong to a higher social class. None of this is at all surprising when we see what happens. It is flattering to the ego to be treated with deference, and in the society portrayed by *Joseph Andrews* people are respectful toward members of the higher classes. Any normal person would hold Lady Booby and Peter Pounce in contempt, but the abnormally virtuous Joseph and Adams treat them with respect. Adams, who "paid all Submission and Deference to his Superiors" in all matters except religion, goes so far as to paint a flattering portrait of Lady Booby (200; 3, 2) and he bows and scrapes when he is offered the opportunity to ride in Pounce's coach (273; 3, 12). The offer of the ride is just an excuse for the repellent man to "communicate his Grandeur" (273; 3, 12), which he does in a manner calculated to insult Adams on grounds of their difference in rank (276; 3, 13). Pounce, we must assume, is not well pleased when Adams replies that he values Pounce's carriage no higher than a "rush" and would have walked if he had known he would be affronted. He then steps out of the moving vehicle.

There are more people like Peter Pounce in this novel who obviously would enjoy it if others bowed and scraped to them. It is a part of the same set of attitudes that when a doctor thinks his patient is of high class, the patient gets star treatment because the doctor hopes that high class means high payment (not that it always did: upper class people were not always rich, and even when they were, they were none too keen to part with their money—which could be why they were rich). Even in more neutral circumstances than these, considerations of class quickly affect the way people think and act: it does not take Wilson long to form "a much higher Opinion of [Fanny's] Quality than it deserved" (quality meant social rank), and he only changes this private opinion when Adams tells him Joseph's story, "not concealing the Meanness of her Birth and Education" (199–200; 3, 2). Adams respects the class of others, while caring nothing for his own. It matters to Adams to include such information. It is the way people think and talk, at least in a Fielding novel, though I think it was probably the way people thought and talked generally in eighteenth-century Britain.

There is no evidence that Fielding is very interested in the classes themselves: his concern ultimately seems to be with the attitudes they engender, in particular hypocrisy. It is a theme of the novel as a whole that these rather absurd attitudes about class generate pride, hypocrisy, and vanity, and they can hurt, as Peter Pounce's pride hurts Adams. Most relevant of all, the behavior that Fielding exposes is a common occurrence. The repugnant hypocrisy of the passengers who want to leave Joseph to die in a ditch constitutes a fine piece of satire, but careful readers also notice that the chapter heading reads: "Containing many surprizing Adventures, which *Joseph Andrews* met with on the Road, scarce credible to those who have never travelled in a Stage-Coach" (51; 1, 12). The verbal formulation (the same as "those who have not seen many Noblemen") suggests that this sort of behavior is in fact commonplace.

Fielding did not portray a class war. I think no one, not even Richardson, did. But *Joseph Andrews* reveals social tensions whose origins lie in class perceptions. It is noticeable that "ladies" (that is, women of some social distinction) are actually jealous of a milkmaid: Fanny's "Under-Lip, according to the Opinion of the Ladies, [was] too pouting. . . . Her Complexion was fair, a little injured by the Sun, but overspread by such a Bloom, that the finest Ladies would have exchanged all their White for it" (152–53; 2, 12). Why, one might wonder, are any ladies even interested in Fanny? One answer is fear, or insecurity, which may lie behind Pamela's rejection of her own class late in the novel, as it lies behind Lady Booby's frustrated entrapment in the fashionable dictates of her own class. In a novel so replete with observations and attitudes based on class, the ladies realize that in the modern world they are in some sense competing with milkmaids. Therefore, to condemn Fanny's underlip as pouting (trivial as that is) is a desperate measure to put down a rival. That is what happens when the old class barriers start to break down.

7

Modern Times and Popular Culture

Joseph Andrews is a response to a rapidly changing world. In literature the most obvious sign of an emergent culture was the novel. Novels were vernacular, not classical; popular, not elitist; middle-class, not highbrow. Fielding was one of the first writers to blend classical and vernacular forms. The result, in *Joseph Andrews,* is a hybrid, a modern novel with classical elements. But this novel is a romance, which means that it belongs to a popular genre with a pedigree going back at least two centuries. In fact, romance is the genre to which Fielding most conspicuously hitched *Joseph Andrews,* because the title page declares: "Written in Imitation of The Manner of Cervantes, Author of Don Quixote." *Joseph Andrews* is really a jumble of genres, but with more romance elements than anything else.

As a culture undergoes major changes, new literary forms usually emerge, but they adopt, absorb, and adapt older forms. The eighteenth century's new literary form, the novel, absorbed obviously older forms of narrative, such as diaries, autobiographies, folk and fairy tales, satiric fictions, travel books, and romances. The novels that paid least attention to these earlier forms were therefore the most innovative, and foremost among them were Samuel Richardson's *Pamela* (1740) and *Clarissa* (1747–48). These were radical novels as far as genre is concerned, yet thoroughly middle class and conservative in their politics. Fielding responded to both these novels, obviously to *Pamela*, by offering the same reading public not just an alternative novel but an alternative form of fiction. A new form paradoxically rooted in tradition, *Joseph Andrews* draws on romance, epic, and the classics.

In this chapter, I propose to explore the connections between the classics and popular culture, indications of modern life such as tastes, fashions, and clothes, what happens when the old and the new meet, and finally what this means for the genre of *Joseph Andrews*.

The typical modern novel of the 1740s did not quote much, if any, Latin or Greek. *Joseph Andrews* has a fair scattering of both languages, and indeed its improbable hero is a learned clergyman who "was frequently at some loss to guess [Slipslop's] meaning, and would have been much less puzzled by an *Arabian* Manuscript" (26; 1, 3). Adams is always quoting bits of Latin and Greek, and he carries with him a manuscript copy of Aeschylus, in Greek, which is spectacularly suspected and misunderstood by one group of boors. Adams is a far cry from Pamela, who is a servant girl with a barely adequate education, to whom Latin and Greek would be only so many hieroglyphs. Indeed, if *Joseph Andrews* has a counterpart to Pamela, it would be Fanny, who is illiterate, or conceivably Pamela's brother, Joseph, who is willing to learn, but is undoubtedly ignorant. Adams's learned accomplishments suggest that Fielding was making a stand in behalf of classical literature. I think that may have been a part of it.

There are allusions to the classics scattered throughout *Joseph Andrews*. There might be something vaguely familiar or at any rate resonant about phrasing like this: "At this Time, an Accident happened which put a stop to these agreeable Walks, which probably would have soon puffed up the Cheeks of Fame, and caused her to blow her brazen Trumpet through the Town, and this was no other than the Death of Sir *Thomas Booby,* who departing this Life, left his disconsolate Lady confined to her House as closely as if she herself had been attacked by some violent Disease" (28–29; 1, 4). The main focus of the sentence is obviously the casual mention of Sir Thomas

Booby's death and the comic reaction it evokes from his "disconsolate" widow. The allusion to Fame and her brass trumpet might easily pass us by, and not just because it is in a subordinate clause. Fame here is a personification that has a direct, but (as it now seems) remote, connection with fame in our modern TV-oriented sense of renown, distinction, and celebrity. Fame used to mean rumor or report, something rather like gossip, and it was personified in Latin literature by "Fama" as a swift-footed young woman who would blow rumors through a trumpet so that everyone would hear them. The trumpet was made of brass to signify that it was indestructible. To put Fielding's sentence another way: soon everyone in London would have heard the rumors about Lady Booby and Joseph walking in the park had not Sir Thomas died, thus forcing her to go through the motions of mourning for him. An editor's footnote does at least alert us to Fielding's allusion to Virgil's *Aeneid*.

I certainly do not propose to explain every classical allusion as laboriously as this. But I do wish to emphasize that it is a common characteristic of Fielding's narrative to incorporate deliberately "lofty" intrusions like this one into what is generally fairly informal English. I think it matters little, at one level, whether or not we recognize the classical allusions, because we can easily recognize a continual shifting of tone, between the "lofty" and the "low."

The classical allusions in *Joseph Andrews* are hardly buried in some way that only an archaeologist could find them: on the contrary, they are obvious because they are so conspicuously different. In one of the most striking and amusing examples, Slipslop declares her passion for Joseph:

> "Yes, *Joseph*, my Eyes whether I would or no, must have declared a Passion I cannot conquer.—Oh! *Joseph!*—"
> As when a hungry Tygress, who long had traversed the Woods in fruitless search, sees within the Reach of her Claws a Lamb, she prepares to leap on her Prey; or as a voracious Pike, of immense Size, surveys through the liquid Element a Roach [a fish, not a bug] or Gudgeon which cannot escape her Jaws, opens them wide to swallow the little Fish: so did Mrs. *Slipslop* prepare to lay her

violent amorous Hands on the poor *Joseph,* when luckily her Mistress's Bell rung, and delivered the intended Martyr from her Clutches. (33–34; 1, 6)

We can hear the change up into the "lofty" language and rhythms of the epic simile, and the change back down again as the incident comes to an end with the banal ringing of a servant's bell. In the "low" language of this novel, water is just plain "water," but in the "lofty" language, water becomes "the liquid Element." We would find phrases like that in *Paradise Lost,* or even James Thomson's *Seasons,* or any number of classical poems, especially epics. One clue to anyone unfamiliar with the classics is that verbal construction, "As . . . so . . . ." In Latin, this is a standard way of introducing a simile, and although it was adopted in English long before Fielding's time, it has a certain foreignness that makes it sound stilted or unnatural to us today. The clue that this alludes to the conventions of classical epic (as opposed to some other kind of classical writing) is that the writer does not confine himself to just one example for his simile. We know that epics are long (by definition) and so we also know that epic poets have plenty of space and leisure at their disposal. Milton does not content himself with saying that the Garden of Eden is better than any other garden you have ever read or heard about: he gives us a whole list, occupying lines and lines of verse, and then tells us that Eden is better than all those other places, and any others you could imagine, and better by far. If we are familiar with the *kind* of literature to which Fielding alludes, so much the better, but if we are not, all is not lost, because we can still hear those changes of tone, and recognize therefore that something absurd is emerging from them. At the very least, Slipslop's passion for Joseph is comic enough as she is about to leap like a huge, hungry, violent animal: that is some love, when what you do is try to leap fiercely on the object of your passion!

If such a classical allusion does escape us, there are numerous actual quotations, in Latin, that do not. Also, it scarcely matters whether or not we understand the Latin when Adams and his latest tormentors cap verses (normally an innocent game in which each player has to quote a line of Latin poetry whose first word begins with the letter that ends the last word of the other player's quotation). That scene is significant not for its quotations but for what it reveals about Adams, about the contrasting ignorance of the other player, who "deserved scourging for his Pronuntiation," and about the corruptibility of the magistrate (146; 2, 11).

There are also places where the narrator quotes from classical sources but gives the gist of the meaning, so that the untrained reader can still make sense of it (170; 2, 15). But most obviously of all, Homer and Virgil, Horace and Ovid are quoted from time to time, either by the narrator or by Parson Adams. Adams tells "the Man of Courage" (who runs away at the first sign of danger) about bravery and cowardice, drawing his examples from Homer, Cicero, Paterculus, and Plutarch (136; 2, 9). The allusions prove no bar to understanding. A typical example of Adams's quotations from the classics in his conversation occurs when he boasts comically to his host at an inn that "the only way of travelling by which any Knowledge is to be acquired" is "in Books"; he thinks he knows more of travel and the world from reading than from actual traveling:

> Do you imagine sailing by different Cities or Countries is travelling? No.
>
> *Coelum non Animum mutant qui trans mare currunt.*
>
> I can go farther in an Afternoon, than you in a Twelve-Month. (181; 2, 17)

It never occurs to Adams to translate his Latin, although nearly everyone who hears his conversation either misunderstands or only partially understands what he says. The same sometimes goes for the narrator's Latin. When he describes Fanny, he warns his reader:

> if thou art of an amorous Hue, I advise thee to skip over the next Paragraph; which to render our History perfect, we are obliged to set down, humbly hoping, that we may escape the Fate of *Pygmalion:* for if it should happen to us or to thee to be struck with this Picture,

we should be perhaps in as helpless a Condition as *Narcissus;* and might say to ourselves, *Quod petis est nusquam.* Or if the finest Features in it should set Lady ---'s Image before our Eyes, we should be still in as bad Situation, and might say to our Desires, *Coelum ipsum petimus stultitia.* (152; 2, 12)

Students reading this passage usually agree that they would say nothing of the sort to themselves, usually do not understand a word of the Latin, and so have trouble understanding the allusion to Narcissus, while Pygmalion is likely to be recognizable as a name only, if at all. This is not of course a slur on students, but a sign of the frustration that quotation and allusion to ancient languages can cause when they are not translated. But we can look at this another way.

Early readers of *Joseph Andrews* included people, particularly women and teenage girls, who understood little or no Latin. They too might have been frustrated by this paragraph, or they might have guessed that such a paragraph was really addressed only to classically educated readers, mostly men. Or, if a description of an illiterate milk-maid is introduced by such relatively elaborate classical apparatus as this, even if we do not understand the apparatus, we might conclude that the narrator may be dealing in incongruity again. Without even knowing a word of the Latin, we might judge that the narrator's description of Fanny is mock-classical. Why would Fielding do such a thing? One answer is that because this is a novel—vernacular, English, unclassical—classically educated readers could be the intended audience, and perhaps Fielding was trying to win them over to the novel as a genre. But we should remember that the very first thing the author says is that "it is possible the mere *English* Reader may have a different Idea of Romance with the Author" (3; preface). The ironic snootiness alerts paltry readers with no Latin that this is, in fact, a book for them.

Classicism and classical allusion in *Joseph Andrews* quickly lead to some consideration of mock-epic, which is a method of using epic, or, as it was usually called then, "heroic," language to describe ordinary, unheroic people, events, and objects (it was not mockery of the epic).[34] The best-known work in this mode, when Fielding was writing, was without doubt Pope's *Dunciad*. This was a long poem that elevated stupid hack writers (at least, Pope portrayed them as stupid) to giddy heights of renown and reward from the goddess Dullness. In the end, universal gloom puts out the light of civilization. Having published the poem in three books in 1728 and 1729, Pope was writing the new fourth and last book in 1741 and then revised the whole poem, possibly at Prior Park, possibly when Fielding himself was there writing *Joseph Andrews*. Pope's mock-epic can be interpreted politically to mean that the forces of darkness are to be found, symbolically, in the mass of junk "literature" then pouring onto the market. The poem can be understood as a critique of the "new" capitalism. This is not the place for a reading of Pope, but I mention the *Dunciad* because Fielding had himself adopted Pope's pseudonym, Martinus Scriblerus,[35] and because this is a poem that resisted the introduction not so much of new literature but of a mass market and the lowering of quality that it caused. *The Dunciad* was also a perfect model, if Fielding wanted one, of a mock-epic that was not designed, as one might expect, to take anything away from epic poetry, but to make modern literature seem appallingly inappropriate if you put it (somehow) in epic language and epic contexts.

Fielding certainly knew about the connection between the publishing industry and popular culture, because he had made his living from 1729 to 1737 as a writer of plays, all of which (with one lost exception) were published as books. Pope really gave us the distinction, which is still bandied about in universities today, between "literature" and "popular literature," or, as one still hears occasionally, "literature" and "trash." Without sharing every one of Pope's rather elitist attitudes, Fielding put into *Joseph Andrews* several observations about what was worth publishing and what was actually published in practice. The most obvious case is Adams, thinking that his own sermons are not just publishable but valuable. His conversation with a bookseller expresses the state of the publishing industry in a capitalist society, where of course the intrinsic value of the product does not determine its price:

Adams . . . was sorry to hear Sermons compared to Plays. "Not by me, I assure you," cry'd the Bookseller, "though I don't know whether the licensing Act may not shortly bring them to the same footing: but I have formerly known a hundred Guineas given for a Play—." "More Shame for those who gave it," cry'd *Barnabas.* "Why so?" said the Bookseller, "for they got hundreds by it." "But is there no difference between conveying good or ill Instructions to Mankind?" said *Adams;* "would not an honest Mind rather lose Money by the one, than gain it by the other?" "If you can find any such, I will not be their Hinderance," answered the Bookseller, "but I think those Persons who get by preaching Sermons, are the properest to lose by printing them: for my part, the Copy that sells best, will always be the best Copy in my Opinion; I am no Enemy to Sermons but because they don't sell. . . ." (80–81; 1, 17)

Aside from the observation that the Licensing Act (the legislation that silenced Fielding the playwright) actually promotes the sale of play texts, there is no obviously pointed satire here. The bookseller's point of view makes perfect commercial sense, and in a commercial world Adams's view of "value" as deriving from moral instruction would be dismissed as mere sentimentalism. The bookseller is not hostile to intrinsic quality (moral or literary), but, because the only value he places on any book is financial, intrinsic quality necessarily becomes a matter of secondary, if not minor, importance. (The eighteenth-century bookseller, incidentally, fulfilled the function of the modern publisher.) Elsewhere, there is a sarcastic remark about "one Bookseller," who "hath *(to encourage Learning and ease the Public)* contrived to give them a Dictionary in this divided Manner [in installments] for only fifteen Shillings more than it would have cost entire" (91; 2, 1), which shows that Fielding was well aware of the tricks by which booksellers maximized their profits.

Fielding had nothing against booksellers, but he disapproved of such self-interested strategies. Similarly, he had nothing against politicians as a breed, but disapproved of the corrupt intrigues of some of them. He had nothing against tradesmen, but disapproved of their manners, which could be a peculiar mixture of obsequiousness and self-importance. Adams praises "the Tradesman, as a very valuable Member of Society, and perhaps inferior to none but the Man of

Learning," but he has just quoted Aristotle, who "proves in his first Chapter of Politics" that trade "is below a Philosopher, and unnatural as it is managed now" (182–83; 2, 17). If trade is unnatural, Fielding presumably means that tradesmen do not always act naturally, and so they behave like Mrs. Slipslop and the doctor; that is, they want to be thought "superior" and so behave accordingly. He therefore satirizes them.

Fielding knew that the targets of his satire had been in existence for a long time—he said 4,000 years (189; 3, 1)—but he took care to place the action of *Joseph Andrews* in a contemporary milieu. That representative of the idle rich, Lady Booby, cannot risk dismissing Mrs. Slipslop because "she had the utmost Tenderness for her Reputation, as she knew on that depended many of the most valuable Blessings of Life; particularly Cards, making Court'sies in public Places, and above all, the Pleasure of demolishing the Reputations of others, in which innocent Amusement she had an extraordinary Delight. She therefore determined to submit to any Insult from a Servant, rather than run a Risque of losing the Title to so many great Privileges" (43–44; 1, 9). This, in short, is modern life for an upper class lady, if she is wealthy. It sounds like being condemned to play Trivial Pursuit for life, and it is meant to associate high fashion with emptiness.

In a similar way, when Lady Booby goes to London, Joseph is promptly exposed to fashion: "His Hair was cut after the newest Fashion, and became his chief Care. He went abroad with it all the Morning in Papers, and drest it out in the Afternoon; they [his fellow servants] could not however teach him to game, swear, drink, nor any other genteel Vice the Town abounded with" (27; 1, 4). The obvious equation of city life with vice is a traditional neurosis, but although London has a certain looming presence in the novel, the city is not the source of vice, only the most obvious place to find it. Parson Trulliber, who has nothing to do with London, is as vicious as anyone who lives there.

The equation that seems to carry more weight for Fielding is that between fashion and vanity. Obviously Parson Adams thinks that anything fashionable is a sign of vanity, but his somewhat severe view more probably causes us to laugh than to concur, especially when he responds to Wilson's account of his earlier life as a wastrel in London:

> "In the Morning [says Wilson] I arose, took my great Stick, and walked out in my green Frock [a long coat] with my Hair in Papers, (*a Groan from* Adams) and sauntered about till ten.
>
> Went to the Auction; told Lady — she had a dirty Face; laughed heartily at something Captain — said; I can't remember what, for I did not very well hear it; whispered Lord — ; bowed to the Duke of — ; and was going to bid for a Snuff-box; but did not, for fear I should have had it.

From	2 to 4, drest myself.	A Groan.
	4 to 6, dined.	A Groan.
	6 to 8, Coffee-house.	
	8 to 9, *Drury-Lane* Play-house.	
	9 to 10, *Lincoln's-Inn-Fields* [another playhouse].	
	10 to 12, Drawing-Room.	A great Groan.

> At all which Places nothing happened worth Remark." At which *Adams* said with some Vehemence, "Sir, this is below the Life of an Animal, hardly above Vegetation; and I am surprized what could lead a Man of your Sense into it." (204–5; 3, 3)

The comedy of Adams's groans seems to compete with his entirely serious moral point: the life Wilson describes here is completely vacuous, devoted as it is to entertainment, gossip, and putting on appearances. But this life, which Wilson has subsequently renounced, is the life of fashion. When we remember that the boor who enjoys "roasting" Adams is also a product of the same fashionable society that trains anything so long as it is not the mind, we might recognize an association between fashion and vanity.

Fashion, by its very nature, is modern: whatever form it takes, fashion is "the latest." Conservatives are always suspicious of fashion, whether it be in hairstyles, clothes, music, or anything else. I have quoted examples of this novel's attitudes to fashion at some length without going into details of the clothing that characters wear (though that repays attention, especially when we contrast anybody's clothes with Adams's torn, muddy, shapeless cassock).[36] But Fielding's main point about fashion appears to be that it is closely associated with behavior that ought to be condemned because it is vain, stupid, or hurtful to others; at any rate, it does not require any effort of the mind. The consequences of addiction to fashion are most obvious in the case of Wilson, whose story thus constitutes an important social theme for the novel.

If fashion, then, is a sign of the modern world—that is, the world Fielding lived in—he does treat that world with suspicion. All the contrasts I have discussed in this chapter suggest a fundamental desire to accommodate the best of the old with the best of the new. A society based on trade is fine if tradespeople will just not mimic the pointless vanity of fashion, and so forth. And the novel is fine if it can be shaped by the best literary traditions: for Fielding, a blend of romance with classical authors such as Horace and Virgil.

Fielding's scattered comments on trade, booksellers, and the like in *Joseph Andrews* point to a fundamental, if somewhat resigned, acceptance of the modern world, of the popular culture whose most conspicuous symbol (at least to a writer) was the novel. Obviously Fielding must have accepted the novel too, because he was writing one, and he did nothing subversive to undermine it. But this novel shows signs of discontent with aspects of that culture, in particular the absurd hypocrisy and the profiteering that it generated. Both of these appear to be essentially selfish in *Joseph Andrews*, and so both of them lie behind the novel's approving emphasis on charity—a social and selfless act, which Martin Battestin sees as one of the twin themes of the novel, and to which I shall return when I discuss money.

8

Sex

Fielding had a healthy attitude toward sex. In fact, glib as it sounds, he often associates sex with health in his fiction. Sexy characters who have satisfying physical relationships usually have a ruddy glow, well-formed muscles, and a "flow of animal spirits" (a phrase from *Tom Jones*). All these characteristics go with sex in *Joseph Andrews:* Joseph is handsome, strong and well-proportioned, and the blood "glowed" in his cheeks (38; 1, 8); and Fanny is plump, "not one of those slender young Women, who seem rather intended to hang up in the Hall of an Anatomist, than for any other Purpose" (152; 2, 12). But the sexual relationship between Joseph and Fanny is all anticipation until the very end, when their wedding night brings them their "exquisite Repast," to which Joseph looks forward with desire, Fanny with "Wishes tempered with Fears" (343; 4, 16). The delaying of actual sexual intercourse between them may, as a narrative tactic, suggest the rhythms of sex itself (an argument borrowed from Roland Barthes), but certainly the delay is paralleled by Adams's insistence that they marry not with a license (which he disapproves) but according to correct form.[37] Adams obliges them, really, to delay their marriage so that religious requirements can be fulfilled, to the letter. The parallel delays have the effect of emphasizing above all their innocence and honesty, and their appreciation of one another's virtues. The result of this is that sex is associated not just with well-formed physiques but also with religion and virtue.

By contrast with them, there is another kind of sexual behavior, or rather another aspect of it, which consists of what I might call illicit or dishonest behavior: lust, rape, or sex that is somehow associated with force or coercion. Fielding's characters tend to display a logic of concupiscence (as I have referred to it elsewhere): that is, their actions often form a pattern that is logical in the sense that sexual desire motivates each step. Whether that logic is Joseph's or Beau Didapper's, sex in *Joseph Andrews* is inseparable from questions of innocence, virtue, and morality. Sex in *Joseph Andrews* is also treated with humor. Fielding knew, instinctively I suppose, and long before Freud, that sex is the basis of numerous jokes that make people laugh. That is not to say that Fielding thinks sex is funny, but rather that he refuses to be solemn or puritanical about it.

It is particularly difficult to discuss sex in *Joseph Andrews* without having *Pamela* at least at the back of one's mind. Joseph is Pamela's brother, and so can be considered the male answer to Pamela's chastity. More substantially than that, although Fielding's novel is not just a commentary on Richardson's, when it comes to sex Fielding proposes a set of attitudes that certainly looks like a measured response to Richardson. First, it is necessary to glance back at what Fielding did with *Pamela* before he came to write *Joseph Andrews*. I am of course referring to *Shamela*.[38] In that hilarious burlesque, Fielding mercilessly parodied just about everything in Richardson's novel: Pamela's materialism, her hypocrisy, her social climbing (what materialism? what hypocrisy? what social climbing? Richardson might have asked). In particular, *Shamela* expresses an attitude that many of Richardson's detractors and parodists shared: Pamela uses her precious virtue as a bargaining chip; her chastity is in effect up for auction to the highest bidder. This point of view therefore denies that Pamela has any real virtue at all, and sees her morality as a fake, a sham, a paper-thin cover for self-serving. As far as sex is concerned, Fielding converts the lofty virtue of Richardson's heroine into a riotous sexual romp, and makes it appear that when she talks of morality or virtue, it is just talk. Fielding's treatment suggests that Richardson's Pamela is really a shameless hussy who wants sex, preferably lots of it, but who disguises her desire with a veneer of hypocritical cant about her virtue.

Not pornographic but certainly bawdy, *Shamela* had perhaps exposed the weakness of Puritan moral orthodoxy, or (some would say) the weakness of middle-class morality. One literary sign of that weakness is the gradual appearance in Britain of pornography—politely called "libertine literature."[39] Pornography had been in existence for centuries, but it began to generate something approaching a mass market between the 1660s and the 1750s, reaching a climax with the publication in 1749 of John Cleland's *Fanny Hill*. The scant surviving evidence suggests that pornographic literature was bought mostly by middle-class Puritans exploiting an eighteenth-century equivalent of the "plain wrapper" to avoid embarrassment. Fielding never comments directly or explicitly on this market, but I am suggesting that *Shamela* indicates an attitude, or a frame of mind, that would condemn such people—not for buying pornography but for pretending that they do not and then piously talking about morality. Pamela talks piously about her virtue; Shamela talks racily about hers. Fielding's pet hate was hypocrisy, and this false piety is a classic manifestation of it.

Since Fielding's major target in *Joseph Andrews* was what he said it was, hypocrisy, we can see his treatment of sex and sexual attitudes as a part of his war on that detestable vice, "the Bane of all Virtue, Morality, and Goodness," as he called it in 1743.[40] Fielding was not in the least interested in describing sexual activity—which is what the pornographer does. In fact, in all his novels, Fielding repeatedly "draws a veil" over sexual action, as he does in *Joseph Andrews* when Fanny waits in bed on the wedding night, and "A Minute carried [Joseph] into her Arms, where we shall leave this happy Couple to enjoy the private Rewards of their Constancy; Rewards so great and sweet, that I apprehend *Joseph* neither envied the noblest Duke, nor *Fanny* the finest Duchess that Night" (343; 4, 16). Fielding's concern was with morality rather than sexual intercourse. Seen in one light, *Joseph Andrews* as a whole revolves around sex: Lady Booby is attracted by Joseph's sexiness, but feels compromised by the class difference between them, and therefore sets the plot in motion; Fanny constantly has to be rescued because some seducer finds her sexually attractive, and therefore she helps to keep the plot moving. Obviously there is far more to the novel—even to the plot—than sex alone, but sex is a crucial ingredient, and a major reason that it is crucial is that it helps to place Fielding's emphasis where he wants it finally: on virtue.

Joseph's virtue seems to be something of an obstacle for modern readers, although there is no very good reason that it should be one. Students today often think that Joseph's virtue is ridiculous, perhaps because virtue does not fare very well in so many sectors of our society. Fielding probably meant Joseph's chastity to be ridiculous, especially because male chastity in such a male-oriented society as Fielding's would seem to be going against the grain. But I find Joseph's clinging to his virtue more ridiculous than the fact that a man protects his chastity, and besides, his chastity means much more to him than Pamela's does to her. Chastity for Pamela seems to mean (or so Fielding evidently thought) only virginity, but for Joseph and Fanny chastity means loyalty as well, which explains why, when circumstances suddenly suggest that they are siblings and that their marriage would be incestuous, "they vowed a perpetual Celibacy, and to live together all their Days, and indulge a *Platonick* Friendship for each other" (335; 4, 15). Their ultimate motive, therefore, is love, not sexual gratification. I would hope there is nothing ridiculous about that.

The comedy, in the sense of sheer fun, associated with Joseph's virtue seems to arise from the contrast between him and the two women who lust after him continually, Lady Booby and Mrs. Slipslop. The successive descriptions of his encounters with them, early in the novel, are comic for his naïveté as much as anything, and it is in one of these early chapters that Fielding slips in the information that Joseph is practically unique because "his Morals remained entirely uncorrupted" in spite of living in such close proximity to all the corrupting fashions of London (27; 1, 4). What follows this remark at once is an account of Lady Booby's machinery (or armory) of seduction, so that yet again fashion and class start to interfere with sex, as they continually do for poor, frustrated Lady Booby. But what really throws her off balance in this scene is Joseph's staunch innocence. There she is trying everything she knows to persuade Joseph to dive into bed with her without her actually having to ask him to do so, and he fails to understand her. It is a classic case of innocence meaning ignorance: he does not even realize he is being seduced. Lady Booby calls it "pretended Innocence" and dismisses him from her presence. She obviously has no idea what to do when she is confronted with genuine innocence, and that is where the comedy lies in this scene (29–30; 1, 5). The scene is virtually replayed twice: once with Slipslop as the hungry tigress, and a second time when Lady Booby confronts him again, this time with a peculiarly inappropriate accusation—that he has made one of the maids pregnant—which she trumps up in order to fire him. This scene includes the "Statue of Surprize" sequence that I quoted in an earlier chapter. Lady Booby is not just furious but utterly astounded that any man, especially one beneath her in rank, should even *have* any virtue, much less assert it. Again, if anything is ridiculous here, it is probably not Joseph's virtue so much as Lady Booby's enraged response to it. I am moved to share a satirist's scorn for her rather than laughter at him.

Joseph's virtue is perhaps no laughing matter. In the coach, the infamous coach, the witless gentleman and the lawyer indulge in various sexual jokes and puns, which are by any normal standards in questionable taste, and "which perhaps gave more Offence to *Joseph* than to any other in the Company" (54; 1, 12). Whether or not Joseph's slightly priggish response is absurd is beside the point. Such casual authorial comments establish a connection between Joseph and moral decency.

What I have suggested so far is that sex is associated with other attributes or concerns: pride, class, lust, virtue, innocence. It is also associated with another of Fielding's recurrent subjects, good nature. What Fielding meant by good nature was very simple: kindness, charity, generosity, cheerful pleasantness in dealing with other people. The embodiment of perfect good nature is Parson Adams, who is, according to Fanny, "the worthiest best natur'd Creature" (292; 4, 5). The mean, selfish, and hypocritical characters in this novel sometimes use "good nature" as a term of scorn, as Pounce does to Adams's face (276; 3, 13), but when the narrator uses it, he means it straightforwardly. Thus the first things we learn about Betty the chambermaid are that "She had Good-nature, Generosity and Compassion," and that she also had "a Flame in her, which required the Care of a Surgeon to cool" (86; 1,18). Superficially at least, Betty's venereal disease, and her sexual appetite—for "Officers of the Army, young Gentlemen travelling the Western Circuit [that is, young lawyers like Fielding himself], inoffensive Squires, and some of the graver Characters," all of whom have been infected by her—probably ought to range her with Mrs. Slipslop or Lady Booby, but not so. Betty is good natured, which cannot be said of those two other worthy ladies, just as it cannot be said of Betty's employer, the harridan Mrs. Tow-wouse. Betty is not the object of any satiric ridicule as, unable to control her passion for Joseph, she leaps on him. If anybody is ridiculous in this comic sense, it is perhaps Joseph himself:

> *Joseph* in great Confusion leapt from her, and told her, he was sorry to see a young Woman cast off all Regard to Modesty: but she had gone too far to recede, and grew so very indecent, that *Joseph* was obliged, contrary to his Inclination, to use some Violence to her, and taking her in his Arms, he shut her out of the Room, and locked the Door.
>
> How ought Man to rejoice, that his Chastity is always in his power, that if he hath sufficient Strength of Mind, he hath always a competent Strength of Body to defend himself: and cannot, like a poor weak Woman, be ravished against his Will. (87; 1, 18)

Perhaps I should modify my remark in any case and suggest that what is ridiculous is not even Joseph, but this last comment of the narrator's. Betty avoids the narrator's condemnation, but why? Why is she any different from Slipslop or Lady Booby? Are they not all lustful?

The are indeed all lustful, but (though this is negative evidence) Betty does not try to suggest that she is anyone's superior; nor does she attempt to conceal her true feelings. More to the point, in the previous chapter she has proven kind and generous to Joseph. Even if sex was her real motive, she at least provides him with tea when he asks for it, which is more than Mrs. Tow-wouse would do. Ultimately, Betty contrasts so glaringly with Mrs. Tow-wouse, who is the obvious satiric target in these scenes, that Betty is bound to come out of the contrast looking preferable to that woman who, the narrator tells us much later, is a composite portrait of "extreme Turbulency of Temper, Avarice, and an Insensibility of human Misery, with a Degree of Hypocrisy" (190; 3, 1).

Betty's passion for Joseph, short-lived and unsuccessful though it is, is honest. More than one critic has pointed out that Fielding is not hard on "crimes" or "sins" involving sex in this way. That is surely right, for there is little to distinguish her antics from those of Slipslop. The real difference, where Fielding is aiming, I think, is that Betty never tries to pass herself off as higher or better. Slipslop's appetite, by contrast, is made to seem almost unnatural, though the fact that she is past childbearing should not make her sexual urge unnatural at all (32; 1, 6). Be that as it may, when Adams blunders into her bedroom he mistakes her at first for a man because his hand brushes against her rough beard, and then he "concluded her to be a Witch, and said he fancied those Breasts gave suck to a Legion of Devils" (332; 4, 14).

Fielding values honesty and openness, combined with loyalty and decency—or virtue—in sexual attitudes and relationships. There is nothing secretive about healthy sex in this novel. On the contrary, at the reunion of Joseph and Fanny (when Fanny has nearly fainted), Joseph "imprinted numberless Kisses on her Lips, without considering who were present," Adams dances with good-natured joy at their happiness, and the narrator tells any prudes who may be reading that if they "are offended at the Lusciousness of this Picture, they may take their Eyes off from it" (155; 2, 12). There are other aspects of sex in *Joseph Andrews* which, though different in emphasis, reinforce the distinction between sex as a healthy and innocent component of a good relationship, and sex as the mere satisfaction of carnal appetite.

Joseph and Fanny are guided in their relationship by a consciousness of virtue. It is worth emphasizing that virtuous characters are not weak or feeble or passive: they are no saps. On the contrary, they are as tough, as robust, and as ready for a fight as the army of rapists and seducers who seem to populate the countryside in this novel. Fanny is rescued from rape three times and Joseph nearly falls victim to rape by Mrs. Slipslop, of all people, twice. Joseph escapes what would be a particularly bizarre fate by happenstance; but Fanny has to be rescued each time by a man who interposes himself violently on her behalf. It is obvious that a virtuous man (Joseph or Adams) fights on her behalf against an unvirtuous assailant; just as obviously, this is a battle between virtue and vice themselves. Joseph's virtue expresses itself as true love—true in that old sense of loyal love of one person—and, in an exactly parallel way, the other men who fancy Fanny express their desire as lust. They may have a variety of reasons for their lust, but the narrator makes it plain that lust is morally indefensible, either by showing the morally correct Adams and Joseph defeating the assailants, or by portraying the assailants themselves as sneering or boorish, or cynical, like the squire who intends to have his way with Fanny by getting Joseph and Adams drunk, and so on. Those who have lustful eyes for Fanny are obviously unattractive characters with scarcely a single redeeming feature. The captain who kidnaps her is plain, straight, unadorned "wicked," and he takes her "to be offered up a Sacrifice to the Lust of a Ravisher," to whom he rudely tells Fanny to yield, "for the 'Squire will be much kinder to you if he enjoys you willingly than by force" (268; 3, 12). The whole scene is irredeemably ugly, and comes to a temporary respite for Fanny only when she is rescued by "a very gallant Person [who] loved a pretty Girl better than any thing, besides his own Money, or the Money of other People" (269; 3, 12): Peter Pounce of course, for whom no one would be able to find a good word.

Lust is also associated with the selfishness that the novel establishes as the hallmark of the fashionable. Wilson's autobiographical story suggests that lust belongs to the same sphere of fashionable life as "an Intrigue" or "the Reputation of it" (203; 3, 3) when he speaks of doing the fashionable things around Covent Garden, where "I shone forth in the Balconies at the Play-houses, visited Whores, made Love to Orange-Wenches, and damned Plays" (206; 3, 3). When Wilson speaks of his contracting and recovering from a venereal disease, his only concern is not becoming infected again: "I found my Passion for Women, which I was afraid to satisfy as I had done, made me very uneasy; I determined therefore to keep a Mistress" (206; 3, 3). He needs an outlet for physical lust, pure and simple. There is not a word of love, nor of virtue, nor of any reason besides the physical why a woman might have attracted him. Wilson's story is instructive for several reasons, one of which is that his wild life in London ranges this sort of sexual appetite among those fashionable vices that the novel continually exposes and satirizes. When Wilson finds happiness, it is with a woman he genuinely loves (222–24; 3, 3).

Lust, then, is immoral, violent, threatening, and fashionable. On the last score, we need only take note of Beau Didapper, one of the "spindle-shanked Beaus" (194; 3, 2) who is not really violent or menacing, even though he lays rude hands on Fanny, who is actually strong enough to repulse him (303; 4, 7). But the beau thinks he can buy Fanny, leaves a servant with her to "make her any Offers whatever," connives with Lady Booby, and tries to deceive Fanny in the dark at night so that he can "enjoy" her (331; 4, 14). Although Didapper is absurd, he is also corrupt (313; 4, 9), but most obviously Lady Booby's "polite Friend" (311; 4, 9, chapter heading) is the epitome of fashionable—or "polite"—society.

Innocence and virtue, which incorporate sexual fidelity—that is, chastity—are the driving forces behind the love of Joseph and Fanny. The sexual relationships of which Fielding approves in this novel are those based on openness, honesty, and respect for someone else's qualities, not just for their bodily attractions. The characters who embody these good qualities are also extremely poor; the lustful are usually rich. In a way, Fielding was putting sex in a social perspective.

9

*V*iolence, *C*rime, *and the* *L*aw

In our era of two world wars, daily acts of international terrorism, urban gang warfare, and 11,000 handgun homicides annually in the United States alone, we might be forgiven for thinking that we have developed a monopoly on violence in the last eighty years. But all things are relative, and it is well to remember that people felt just as insecure in eighteenth-century Britain, which was a violent place without even the benefit of a police force until Fielding and his half-brother founded one in London in 1750. Britain may not have been constantly as uproarious as an engraving by Hogarth, but neither was it the placid, pastel place portrayed in the paintings of Gainsborough and Reynolds. In early eighteenth-century London one criminal, Jonathan Wild, was as great a celebrity as the prime minister, everyone knew who Jack Sheppard was, and John Gay wrote an opera whose characters are thieves and whores and whose hero is a highway robber: *The Beggar's Opera* broke all box office records.

Violent crime was certainly common, and violence in noncriminal senses was common also, especially in the cities. One of Fielding's most interesting essays is his *Enquiry into the Causes of the late Increase of Robbers* (1751), in which he predicted that this "evil" would get worse: "the streets of this town [London], and the roads leading to it, will shortly be impassable without the utmost hazard; nor are we threatened with seeing less dangerous gangs of rogues among us, than those which the Italians call the Banditti."[41] It may seem curious that Fielding laid the blame for the alarming increase in robbery squarely at the door of the idle rich. The rate and increase of serious crime are impossible to measure, but it is certain that laws protecting property, and the prolific consumption of gin in the 1730s had much to do with the period's most typical crime, theft.

There is one respect in which Fielding's novels resemble Defoe's. They incorporate extensive commentary on the crimes and the violence of his society, ranging from armed robbery, which occurs in each one of Fielding's novels, to sheep stealing, petty larceny, and a pitched battle in a churchyard (in *Tom Jones*). It is this level of criminal violence that enters Fielding's fiction, rather than war, which must seem more remote when your country's navy is fighting with Spain's 4,000 miles away and the newspaper reports of battles are weeks out of date. Fielding does, however, incorporate an awareness of war in his novels, including *Joseph Andrews;* for example, the brief allusion to the British forces' disastrous defeat at Cartagena in 1741 (131; 2, 7), but, like the brief comments on the *Daily Gazetteer* (183; 2, 17), the allusion serves mainly to create a contemporary context for the narrative.

Violence in *Joseph Andrews* is predominantly of the social (as opposed to the international) kind. One of the best examples is the attack on Joseph. Dismissed from Lady Booby's service, and still wearing his livery, Joseph stops at his first inn to take shelter from "A violent Storm of Hail" (50; 1, 11). The very next incident after his leaving the inn is the armed robbery that leads to the stagecoach scene. Joseph knocks one of the highwaymen down, but is felled himself when the other cracks him on the head with a pistol butt. Fielding is not concerned with the painfulness of such blows, but with the violence that is prompted by malice: "The Thief, who had been knocked down, had now recovered himself; and both together fell to be-labouring poor *Joseph* with their Sticks, till they were convinced they had put an end to his miserable Being: They then stript him entirely naked, threw him into a Ditch, and departed with their Booty" (51–52; 1, 12). There is more to this scene than the routine occurrence of highway robbery, and more to it even than the suffering of an unfortunate victim of violent crime. This part of the scene introduces the hypocrisy of the travelers in the stagecoach, which is the focus of the chapter as a whole, but the violence done to Joseph, which he returns in kind for as long as he is conscious, also confirms that he is a reasonable, decent, and naive young man. Confronted by the thieves, he is "ordered to stand and deliver. He readily gave them all the Money he had, which was somewhat less than two Pounds; and told them he hoped they would be so generous as to return him a few Shillings, to defray his Charges on his way home." They of course reply "with an Oath, *Yes, we'll give you something presently: but first strip and be d—mn'd to you.—Strip,* cry'd the other, *or I'll blow your Brains to the Devil*" (51; 1, 12). Joseph naively asks if they will not take his coat (which is borrowed, so it is not his to give, but he does not tell them that) because of the cold. They proceed to attack him.

There is in this scene evidence of the naïveté of the innocent victim, but also of the mindless, antisocial hostility of the thieves. Their primary and ostensible purpose is to take money and property, but their secondary and perhaps unconscious purpose is to hurt and damage. I am reminded of the urban legend of the New Yorker who puts in his car a sign that reads "No radio in this car," only to find his vehicle vandalized and his sign annotated "Get one." Such behavior, condemned by society as criminal of course, seems to be evidence of an uncivilized ferocity, a kind of hatred. In beating Joseph, as they think, nearly to death, Fielding's thieves display a level of violence that their situation does not require or justify, not even to two such simpleminded thugs. Their attack on Joseph is provoked by his naïveté (which he thinks is reasonableness), his failure to understand that they arrogate to themselves the illegal right to take *all* his property. Their reaction is paralleled by Trulliber, who threatens violence when Adams tells him, reasonably (if naively in the circumstances), that he is no Christian because he has no charity (167–68; 2, 14).

The robbery of Joseph's money and clothes exemplifies violence as a social problem, to which neither Fielding nor anyone else has a practical solution. One reason for the absence of a solution is the failure of the judicial system to address the problem. This was an issue that came to dominate Fielding's later writing—especially *Amelia*—but even in *Joseph Andrews* he affords us glimpses of the perversion of the law far beyond the mere irritant of a pettifogger like Scout (248–85; 4, 3). There is little chance of discouraging (or apprehending or prosecuting) a criminal when the processes of arrest and examination by a magistrate are so arbitrary and so open to abuse. One ignorant and stupid magistrate does not bother to read any deposition, but prepares to send Adams to jail to await trial simply because he has been accused, and then when Mr. Booby unexpectedly turns up and vouches for Adams as "a Gentleman of a very good Character" (149; 2, 11), the magistrate is just as quick to change his tactics and release him. What persuades him to do this is the simple fact that Booby has authority because he is a squire, and he says the magic word, "Gentleman." Justice is therefore the servant of "interest" and class.

Fielding links perverted justice (and unfair laws) with crime, violence, hypocrisy, and self-interest. Knowing that justice will not be done whatever the crime, Fielding suggests—in the single chapter incorporating the violent assault and the hypocrisy of the stagecoach passengers and Mrs. Tow-wouse—that the really serious underlying social problem is a larger one: the absence of human decency.

Most of the violent episodes in *Joseph Andrews* are nowhere near as heavy with implications as this one, because violence is absolutely commonplace in the novel's world. Fielding's characters never tap gently at a door (unless they are eavesdropping), they bang it violently with a fist or a stick; most of them do not speak softly, they shout; they do not come to negotiated settlements over disagreements, they clang and bash each other with resonant implements such as saucepans. Arguments end in uproar, and even love for someone is a violent affection. Each time Fanny is threatened with rape—itself of course an act of appalling violence—she is rescued by the violent intervention of Joseph or Adams. Fielding's fictional world is a noisy environment where people fall or are knocked down, and the thing that most commonly gets broken is a skull. Fighting is a normal occurrence. Even the weather is violent: people stop at inns to shelter from violent storms and showers. Physical violence and noise are so common in *Joseph Andrews* that they become the milieu in which the characters move.

Although criminal violence is malicious and harmful in *Joseph Andrews,* noncriminal violence is resolved, as often as not, with good humor. The fights come to an end, and all warring parties calm down, or agree to suppress their differences, or the characters just go their separate ways. Even if Fielding sometimes uses violence for comic effect, it is still extreme, just as it was in real life. Joseph hits Didapper's servant so hard he nearly kills him, Adams likewise nearly kills Slipslop, and so on.

Probably the most memorable scenes in the novel are the fights, the near-rapes, the farcical bedroom scenes at the end, and the moments of physical humor when Adams tries to catch Trulliber's pig, when he outruns a horse, or when he leaps from a moving coach. As the travelers take to the road they meet a succession of people who confront them with violence of one sort or another. Violence takes the form of physical assault, heated arguments (which sometimes develop into fights), and loud, shouting voices. An argument between Mr. Tow-wouse and the man who poses as learned is interrupted by "a mighty Noise" (63–64; 1, 14). A little later, the hypocritical Parson Barnabas tries to free himself from the company of Adams by "ringing with all the Violence imaginable," because he thinks Adams no better than the Devil, to which Adams responds with blank incomprehension that he did not know he was giving offense (83–84; 1, 17). The hog's pudding episode, which is "A dreadful Quarrel" anyway (118; 2, 5, chapter heading), is violent from start to finish, but it begins as a clash of personalities really: the surly host, "who always proportioned his Respect to the Appearance of a Traveller," thoughtlessly yells at his wife for rubbing a mere footman's wounded leg, "At which Words, she fell to chafing more violently" (119; 2, 5). When Joseph tells this stupid and selfish man that the shabby Adams is one of his "Betters," he tries at once "to lay violent Hands on him" (119; 2, 5). The fight that ensues is noisy and messy. The violence is associated primarily with boorish behavior—in this case that of a man who "was indeed perfect Master of his House and every thing in it but his Guests" (119; 2, 5). This is a pattern that Fielding develops, sometimes as extensively as in this scene, sometimes only in passing, as when that gentleman who talks grandly about courage speaks "with so violent a Gesture, so loud a Voice, so strong an Accent, and so fierce a Countenance," that he would have frightened anyone but Adams (132; 2, 7). Within a few pages Fielding plunges Adams into another violent encounter, in which he "levelled a Blow" with his crab stick at the head of one of Fanny's ravishers, and would have killed him had he not had a particularly thick skull (137; 2, 9). Fielding takes the opportunity to have some mock-epic fun at the expense of this brainless individual.

Amid all the shouting and fighting, some patterns begin to emerge. Aside from the now obvious fact that violence is normal in the kind of society that this novel emphatically portrays, the novel reveals that two good Christians fight—there is nothing passive about them—and that violence helps to confirm the distinctions of personality and morality between Fielding's virtuous characters and his vicious ones.

It is worth noticing that the socially superior characters as well as the thieves and boors also normally engage in physically violent actions, if not always as a matter of course. They may dress nicely and affect to be delicate in their tastes and manners, but they have grosser physical appetites and are prepared to lower their dignity to satisfy them. Beau Didapper, the polite "little Person" (he is only 4 feet 5 inches) "or rather Thing that hopped after Lady *Booby*" is quite willing to use violence even though he is upper class (313; 4, 9). Like Fanny's other "admirers," who ravish, attack, and so forth, this pathetic social butterfly leaps on Fanny when there is no one but his retinue of servants around to watch, but in public he goes only so far as to offer "a Rudeness to [Fanny] with his Hands," that is, he makes a pass at her (320; 4, 11). He is boxed on the ear for his trouble, and promptly draws his sword, but Lady Booby intervenes to prevent any further violence. Admittedly these characters (Peter Pounce, too) try first to get their way by hints (not necessarily subtle ones) and bribes and promises rather than by physical violence. Since the fights are such undignified affairs, those with social pretensions and aspirations would presumably not want to become involved in anything so sordid as a scuffle. And given the structure of the relations between characters in the novel as a whole, one might have expected that physical methods would be associated with the socially low, and verbal ones with the socially high, but Fielding does not use violence as a theme in this way. His emphasis appears instead to suggest that everyone in this society has a tendency to be violent. This is true, if somewhat indirectly, even of Lady Booby: although she "carelessly" drapes a hand on Joseph (39; 1, 8), her reaction to his apology is to fly "into a violent Passion, and refusing to hear more, ordered him instantly to leave the Room" (42; 1, 8). She then questions "this violent Passion" and rings the bell for Slipslop "with infinite more Violence than was necessary" (42; 1, 8).

What distinguishes the characters in this context of violence appears to be a simple matter of motives. Typical of the violent scenes in the novel as a whole, these scenes show that the good Adams is just as capable of violent action as those who yell and hit or rob other people. Trulliber clenches his fist when Adams reprimands him for his boorish lack of charity (168; 2, 14), but Adams himself shows his support for Joseph by "clenching a Fist rather less than the Knuckle of an Ox" (67; 1, 15), and he threatens similar violence to a surly, deliberately unhelpful fellow (96; 2, 2). When the Wilson family's dog dies because the local squire has shot him, Adams immediately "grasped his Crab Stick, and would have sallied out after the Squire, had not *Joseph* with-held him" (228; 3, 4). The obvious point is that Adams and Joseph use violence as a last resort to defend themselves against attack, but they never initiate it. Fielding seems to approve even revenge, since Joseph gives the repulsive captain "a most severe Drubbing, and ended with telling him, he had now had some Revenge for what his dear *Fanny* had suffered" (271; 3, 12). He races to rescue Fanny from yet another "attack" by dealing the latest rapist (the one who turns out to be Beau Didapper's servant) "so lusty a Blow in that part of his Neck which a Rope would have become with the utmost Propriety, that the Fellow staggered backwards," and then knocks out three of the man's teeth, which is at least preferable to the death this blow would have caused had it not been deflected (304; 4, 7). Another major fight ensues. Joseph and Adams are certainly never feeble. For one thing, they are built powerfully and are good at boxing; Adams prevents yet more violence when he "confined [Mrs. Tow-wouse's] Arms with the Strength of a Wrist, which *Hercules* would not have been ashamed of" (85; 1, 17). Adams and Joseph do not turn the other cheek, but fight back. Their Christianity is, as one might say, athletic. They are prepared to live by the morality which dictates that whoever starts a fight is in the wrong and should not get away with it. And if the aggressor is also stupid, or boorish, or morally degenerate, he deserves all the violence he gets.

Violence confirms the distinctions between characters in the simplest of ways. The aggressors are hostile by definition, but their hostility is usually motivated by some trait that is ugly or reprehensible. Lust, greed, selfishness, or simple malevolence are the typical causes. The result is that there is a cast of predators waiting for their prey. The difference between Joseph and the two thieves who strip him is really rather obvious: his naive virtue comes up against their vice. But the difference between Joseph and, say, Mrs. Tow-wouse is less conspicuous, perhaps because Fielding presents it to his readers in a less concentrated form. It is easy enough to see the contrast between Joseph's almost instinctive inclination to be charitable and this ghastly woman's selfish refusal to give anybody anything or part with a farthing. This landlady's rejection of charity and her ill-tempered demand that Joseph should not be given a shirt appear last in the sequence after the two robbers and the stagecoach travelers. But in the context of violence, and, more specifically, noise, she has a dreadfully "loud and hoarse" voice (62; 1, 14), which is perfectly suited to her physical ugliness and her vile temper. Her voice rises above "a most hideous Uproar ... like a Bass Viol in a Concert ... clearly and distinctly distinguished among the rest" (84; 1, 17). The quality of voices is a simple metaphor that Fielding uses, here and elsewhere, to suggest or reflect character. By contrast with the characters who roar, Joseph has a "sweet" voice. One of the first things Fielding tells us about him is that "his Voice being so extremely musical, that it rather allured the Birds than terrified them," he was transferred to the huntsman, whose dogs likewise preferred "the Melody of his chiding to all the alluring notes" of the hunting horn (21–22; 1, 2). A soft and melodious voice thus signifies a kind, charitable, honest, decent character. Noise and loud voices are associated with the vices of the basically unpleasant characters.

Violence and noise are facts of life. They are not desirable, but violence at least is sometimes necessary, in circumstances calling for self-defense.

10

Religion

Samuel Johnson (who, by the way, declared with his blunt defiance, "I, indeed, never read *Joseph Andrews*") defined "religion" in his great *Dictionary of the English Language* (1755) as "Virtue, as founded upon reverence of God, and expectation of future rewards and punishments." There, in clear, simple, straightforward, accessible language, is the ordinary eighteenth-century Englishman's attitude to religion. Religion is Christian virtue. That is just about Fielding's attitude, too. The trouble is, it is not very specific. But that need not be a problem, in fact.

Drawing mostly on Fielding's essays in the *Champion* (1739–41), James A. Work concluded that Fielding was the major moralist of his day, determined to preach Christianity as a solution to social problems. That may be overstating the case, but Work seems to have been right in classing Fielding generally among the conservative, Low Church Christians.[42] In a very English way, Fielding had a rational, somewhat freewheeling, easy-come-easy-go attitude to religion. He thought one should respectfully acknowledge the existence of a God and go to church, but he cared little about formal doctrine, even less about forms of worship and prayer. He thought it far more important to express one's religious duty in everyday social situations, to be kind to other people, to help them out of tight spots if you could, to lend them money if they were poor, to share your food with them if they were hungry, in any event to do something rather than talk piously. When we talk about religion in *Joseph Andrews* we are not talking about altars, hymns, or prayers, but rather about a system of ethics governed by a simple concept of a providential deity. True, there is mention of sermons, and we actually hear something like a part of one sermon, but religion in this novel does not depend on such evidence. Fielding's treatment of religion almost entirely avoids any consideration of doctrines or forms of worship. Instead, he concentrates on how people live their lives, which amounts to concentrating on morality. Adams, in particular, serves God first and his fellow men second. The repeated emphasis on Providence, which is reflected in the idea of the author controlling his narrative, reveals a fundamental optimism because it posits a benevolent deity who ensures that the world is ultimately harmonious.

One of the quotations Johnson used to illustrate his definition of religion was from Robert South: "If we consider it as directed against God, it is a breach of *religion;* if as to men, it is an offence against morality." That suggests that religion and morality are two sides of the same coin. As it happens, Fielding's own sense of religion was shaped by the kind of thinking that could be found in the sermons of South and also those of Isaac Barrow, John Tillotson, and Benjamin Hoadly. Fielding may not have prepared to write his novel by reading the works of these so-called latitudinarian divines, but there is not much doubt that he was familiar with the religion they preached, and that it was a religion he approved, difficult though it is to define exactly. He owned copies of their books, though some of them he acquired after writing *Joseph Andrews*.[43] Fielding was not one to attach himself to an "ism," but he shared many of the attitudes expressed by these men: if that means that Fielding embraced latitudinarianism, then so be it.

As Battestin quite rightly points out, Fielding preferred to laugh rather than preach about the follies and vanities of men and women,[44] and so the religious content of *Joseph Andrews* tends to be rooted in the satiric clash between virtue and vice: between a virtuous but unwordly clergyman and a hypocritical and worldly one; or between a virtuous footman and a greedy lawyer. Since the moral victory is awarded every time to the virtuous characters, we are reading the fictional triumph of religion in a fictional world, which, like the real world, is dominated by an almost pathological greed for money and the selfishness and power that go with it. Combined with what I take to be this novel's satiric mode, religion therefore emerges as something to be championed—not just defended, but championed, in particular by two amiable but tough-minded men who are willing to fight for their principles.

Like other aspects of *Joseph Andrews,* such as its humor and its mock-epic apparatus, religion as a theme incorporates modern English and ancient, pre-Christian Rome. Such an apparent paradox is quite normal anyway in eighteenth-century writing. Any student who has read Milton knows that the greatest Christian poem in the English language owes enormous debts in all kinds of ways to pre-Christian authors. Now, in Fielding's time, seventy years after Milton's death, Horace was still being quoted just as often as Saint Paul (perhaps more often) as an authority on matters of ethics. The whole pastoral tradition—on which *Joseph Andrews,* like *Paradise Lost,* depends in part—is fundamentally pagan, but it gradually gathered Christianizing additions.[45] For a peculiarly striking example of the dominance of classical culture in a supposedly Christian society, all we need to do is look at *Gulliver's Travels,* part 3, where Gulliver, that ordinary but terribly fallible Englishman, enjoys the unusual privilege of meeting people who died long ago. He lists six great names: Brutus, Junius, Socrates, Epaminondas, Cato the Younger, and Sir Thomas More. These men constitute a *"Sextumvirate* to which all the Ages of the World cannot add a Seventh."[46] Three Romans, two Greeks, and an English martyr. What about Jesus Christ? And this is in a book written by a Church of England clergyman.

Fielding puts into *Joseph Andrews* rather less of the pagan classics than Swift and Pope habitually incorporated in their writing. Yet *Jo-*

seph Andrews blends Christian and classical. To start with, Joseph's name recalls Joseph from the Bible—specifically Genesis 39. As Battestin observes, Fielding made this allusion very conspicuous in a grammatically insignificant place (rather like having Sir Thomas Booby die in a casual clause in the previous sentence): Lady Booby "ordered *Joey,* whom for a good Reason we shall hereafter call JOSEPH . . . to her, bad him sit down, and having accidentally laid her hand on his, she asked him *if he had never been in Love?*" (29; 1, 5).[47] Fielding's technique indicates not just the trivial fact that the childish, familiar name Joey is to be dropped now; he also tells us he has a good reason to use the full name, which is printed in capital letters. Before the sentence is out, Lady Booby is trying to seduce Joseph. People familiar with the Old Testament today (like most, if not all, of Fielding's earliest readers) recognize that the attempted seduction of Joseph by Lady Booby is a parallel, ludicrous though it may be, of the biblical story of the attempted seduction of Joseph by the wife of Potiphar, and Joseph's rejection of her. Joseph alludes to this again, and even more glaringly, when he tells Pamela "I hope I shall copy your Example, and that of *Joseph,* my Name's-sake; and maintain my Virtue against all Temptations" (47; 1, 10). The implied morality of the novel is, without a shadow of a doubt, derived from the morality of that biblical episode. At the same time, the two heroes of the novel are on a journey that we may call a Christian pilgrimage or a classical odyssey, according to taste. (I tend to think they are the same thing— a journey of discovery and self-discovery—in different costumes.) Yet in addition to the rather obvious biblical allusion, Fielding's acknowledged debt to *Don Quixote* is even more relevant in explaining the shape (some would say lack of shape) of the episodic narrative than any very precise Christian or classical intent. What we are left with in a case like this is not a muddle, but certainly a blending of elements that masks the origin of each individual component.

In much the same manner of blending, Fielding incorporates in the Wilson episode the ideal of retirement from the vanities and materialism of the city. That ideal is predominantly classical, but not specifically biblical or otherwise Christian. Yet Wilson and his family are models of charity and neighborliness, "for they had nothing which those who wanted it were not welcome to" (228; 3, 4). In the novel's religious frame of reference, the Wilsons are good Christians who yet prompt Adams to declare "that this was the Manner in which the People had lived in the Golden Age" (229; 3, 4).[48]

Like Joseph, Fielding's parson is suggestively named, after both Abraham and Adam, but instead of being a precise biblical model, Parson Adams is a classical scholar who takes Aeschylus on his travels, knows the drama of Aristophanes, Euripides, and Sophocles, and discourses (with lengthy quotations from memory) so learnedly on Homer that Wilson "now doubted whether he had not a Bishop in his House" (198–99; 3, 2). Wilson's response shows that it would apparently be normal for a learned clergyman to be entirely familiar with the pre-Christian classics and, like Adams, to use them as models of morality as well as literature. When in raptures over the *Iliad*, "this divine Poem" (198; 3, 2), Adams emphasizes the poem's brilliance in depicting the infinite variety of human nature, so much so that he is "convinced, the Poet had the worthiest and best Heart imaginable" (199; 3, 2). That is what Adams values most of all: a worthy and good heart. It is what Fielding grew accustomed to call good nature. Adams does not care what a man's formal religion is so long as he is generous, hospitable, and charitable. His opinion "hath always been, that a virtuous and good *Turk*, or Heathen, are more acceptable in the sight of their Creator, than a vicious and wicked Christian, tho' his Faith was as perfectly Orthodox as St. *Paul's* himself" (82; 1, 17). This is the keynote of the entire treatment of religion in *Joseph Andrews*. Religion is not doctrinaire, and the classics have much to teach us about human nature and civilized values. Only the corrupt or degenerate clergymen, Barnabas and Trulliber, oppose Adams's view and condemn him as irreligious. Even Joseph seems to know far more about being a good Christian (as this novel defines it) than Parson Barnabas, who should know better. Since Barnabas and Trulliber are demonstrably irreligious themselves, Adams and his religion come out of the dramatized conflict triumphant.

What we see repeatedly in the adventures is confrontation between honesty and hypocrisy, and it is usually expressed as a conflict between the charitable and the uncharitable, rather than some conflict between one religion and another. In fact, Adams agrees in large part with a Catholic priest (traveling incognito because of Britain's punitive anti-Catholic laws). The charitable characters, including the pedlar, one trusting innkeeper, the Wilson family, and the three travelers contrast so obviously with the likes of Peter Pounce, who withholds the servants' wages (47; 1, 10), or Mrs. Tow-wouse, whose eyes water at the sight of a gold coin (95; 2, 2), that charity sometimes seems to be the test of morality in the novel. Battestin is surely right when he argues that charity and chastity, the twin virtues espoused by latitudinarianism, are the twin virtues of this novel too. Because I have discussed chastity (although in a different light) in an earlier chapter, I will deal only with charity here.

From the simplest material point of view, the major problem facing Adams, Joseph, and Fanny is that they never have enough money. At a moment of great joy for Adams, when he offers his hospitality to the two young people and they have all enjoyed "perfect Happiness over a homely Meal" (278; 4, 1), his wife reminds him tartly that "he had probably ruined his Family with his foolish Tricks" (322; 4, 11). Then his daughter continues:

> "Indeed Father, it is very hard to bring Strangers here to eat your Children's Bread out of their Mouths. You have kept them ever since they came home; and for any thing I see to the contrary may keep them a Month longer: Are you oblig'd to give her Meat, tho'f she was never so handsome? . . . I would not give such a Vagabond Slut a Halfpenny, tho' I had a Million of Money; no, tho' she was starving." "Indeed but I would," cries little *Dick;* "and Father, rather than poor *Fanny* shall be starved, I will give her all this Bread and Cheese."—(*Offering what he held in his Hand.*)—*Adams* smiled on the Boy, and told him he rejoiced to see he was a Christian; and that if he had a Halfpenny in his Pocket he would have given it him; telling him, it was his Duty to look upon all his Neighbours as his Brothers and Sisters, and love them accordingly. (322– 23; 4, 11)

The scene reveals that Adams has not succeeded in inculcating his principle into his own daughter, though that is a point Fielding neither emphasizes nor develops. The major point of this scene is that, for Adams, being a Christian is being charitable: giving and sharing whatever you have with those who are less well provided for. Adams is ready to return money to Wilson because he thinks it must have been given in error. As soon as Joseph convinces Adams that Wilson must have given him the money intentionally, Adams applauds Wilson "not so much for the Conveniency which it brought them, as for the sake of the Doer, whose Reward would be great in Heaven" (233; 3, 5). That is how Adams lives his own life: he has little to give, but gives it all the same, which is what his wife, "who was a very good sort of Woman, only rather too strict in Œconomicks" (323; 4, 11), complains about.

Adams runs into difficulty in the numerous situations in the novel where he expects other people to behave as he does. He continually expects others to pay his bills when he has no money. Students, I find, commonly condemn Adams for this, and say that he should not accept what he cannot afford. But he can be defended. He is not taking anything by deception (which is the main objection to his behavior), because Fielding supplies us with copious evidence that Adams is incapable of deceit, wholly absentminded, and too committed to the idea of congenial conversation over a pitcher of beer even to think about who will pay for it (255; 3, 8). He may be stupid—though naive would be the better word—but he is not a freeloader. And in an important respect, his assumption that others will behave as he does is well placed, because although he is wrong, more worldly people than he make exactly the same assumption. It is in fact the way of the world: if you are a conniving schemer, then apparently you expect everybody else to be a conniving schemer too, and you regulate your own conduct accordingly. The defense of Adams does not rest there, though it could. These episodes reach seemingly impossible impasses as bills mount up and there is nothing to pay them with, but if we look at how each problem is resolved, we see that Fielding's concern is with charity and trust, not deceit. My favorite is the strangely eloquent, poignant one that looks like a parody of a page from a Defoe novel:

Mr. *Adams* and Company D^r	0	7	0
In Mr. *Adams's* Pocket, -----------------------------------	0	0	6½
In Mr. *Joseph's*, ---	0	0	0
In Mrs. *Fanny's*, ---	0	0	0
Balance ---	0	6	5½

This scene (in 2, 13) is placed very carefully between two instances of repugnant behavior. The first is Slipslop's refusal to recognize Fanny because to do so would compromise her own self-importance. Adams "knew no more of all this than the Cat which sat on the Table, imagining Mrs. *Slipslop's* Memory had been much worse than it really was" (158; 2, 13). This is confirmation, hardly needed by this stage of the novel, that Adams has no means of recognizing hypocrisy. The second incident, after the bill is presented, is that Adams goes off to ask for the money from the wealthy Parson Trulliber, who treats him like dirt, deliberately gives him "a little of the worst Ale" (163; 2, 14), eats greedily and selfishly, and of course refuses to give Adams a penny. The bill at the inn is a device that enables Fielding to reflect on self-centered rudeness. The reason why the travelers have no money in the first place is that Fanny's purse has been stolen, and the fellow who took it, says Fielding with his customary irony, "had unluckily forgot to return it" (161; 2, 13). This is not a basis for a discourse on theft, nor poverty, nor even "the immense Quantity of Ale which Mr. *Adams* poured in" (161; 2, 13); it is the basis for Fielding's portrayal of the vices of vanity and meanness.

Vanity and meanness and the love of wealth do of course find their way, incongruously enough, into organized religion, as one or two TV "religions" have revealed in recent years. Only one religious doctrine is singled out for satiric treatment in *Joseph Andrews*, and that is Methodism, which Fielding condemns (by way of Adams and, to a lesser extent, Joseph) because he perceives it to attach too much importance to forms of worship and too little to good works (81–83;

1, 17). *Shamela* had attacked Methodism's principal leaders, George Whitefield and (to a lesser extent) John Wesley, for the same reason and with more gusto. Adams contrasts with the objectionable clergymen who prefer to accumulate wealth rather than to comfort the sick or preach, but his belief in practical charity, in good works, contrasts with the formal doctrine of Methodism too. This was another sign of the modern world, since Methodism had been founded as recently as 1739. To Fielding, Whitefield's doctrine of faith and grace meant a religion that could keep the conscience clean without requiring a single good deed. Though no expert, Joseph knows that Methodism is deficient, when he writes to tell his sister that Lady Booby has fallen in love with him, "That is, what great Folks call falling in love, she has a mind to ruin me; but I hope, I shall have more Resolution and more Grace than to part with my Virtue to any Lady upon Earth" (46; 1, 10). Where a Methodist would supposedly rely on grace, Joseph intends to preserve his virtue by more pragmatic means. Joseph goes on to explain that, as Adams has taught him, chastity is a "great" virtue in a man or a woman, and it is here that he defines chastity not as anything prim or laughable but as sexual fidelity, and since that will be within marriage, chastity also means monogamy. The somewhat sly implication is that Methodism (and *Pamela* for that matter) is associated with some sort of loose sexuality, as well as with hypocrisy.

Because religion is virtue, religion is in *Joseph Andrews* a matter of ethical behavior. It is especially a matter of rejecting hypocrisy and vanity, which Fielding tells us in his preface to the whole novel are the two sources of affectation—being self-important and so forth—which is in turn "the only Source of the true Ridiculous" (7; preface). Hypocrisy and vanity are satirically exposed in a succession of innkeepers, snobs, lawyers, doctors, beaux, fine ladies, . . . and clergymen. Since Adams contrasts with all these people and is obviously virtuous, his religion is the one the novel recommends. He is unorthodox and undoctrinaire, untainted by corruption, honest to a fault, and not usually inclined to preach except from the pulpit, though he does always carry a sermon with him "for fear what may happen" (250; 3, 7).

Above all, Adams's religion shows that there is no question of the perfectibility of human nature. In a famous scene, Adams commends Stoic resignation when some disaster befalls us: that is his response to the unwelcome news (false, as it turns out) that Fanny and Joseph are siblings, which plunges these two into despair. "When any Accident threatens us," he warns, "we are not to despair, nor when it overtakes us, to grieve" (308; 4, 8), for it is Adams's Christian belief that "Despair is sinful" (217; 3, 3). Within moments, he himself receives an equally false report that his son has drowned: "He stood silent a moment, and soon began to stamp about the Room and deplore his Loss with the bitterest Agony" (309; 4, 8). Among the many things to be learned from this scene, one is that Adams is imperfect. We know that he is vain about his own achievements as a schoolteacher (230–32; 3, 5), and that he thinks he has successfully taught his little boy Latin, but he has not. He does not practice what he preaches, at least not in some circumstances. While this comes dangerously close to hypocrisy, it is finally not hypocrisy, because Adams has no self-interest at stake. Ultimately, that is what marks him and his religion as so commendable. He never has any self-interest at stake; he is unpolitical; he puts God above all human affairs, and he submits to Providence—or rather, he tries to. All this is not to say that Adams's religion would work or does work in the real world—it seems to be so impractical that Fielding could not possibly be suggesting such a thing—but it shows a standard of human decency and fraternity from which the modern world, governed by the institutionalized self-interest system that Fielding calls the ladder of dependence, has fallen.

11

Money

Money is always likely to be on your mind if you do not have any. Money was certainly on Fielding's mind in the years leading up to *Joseph Andrews*. With debts looming over him and his family, Fielding accepted money—it may have been a bribe, but the circumstances are still murky—from Sir Robert Walpole. The general supposition is that Walpole paid Fielding not to publish *Jonathan Wild*, which satirizes "great men" like Walpole in the person of a notorious criminal. Peter Pounce makes a fleeting appearance there too. Fielding must also have been relieved when his publisher, Andrew Millar, paid him £183 for *Joseph Andrews*, but before the year was out he had been sued for £197. Like Defoe, Fielding knew what it was like to be continually in debt, and he put some of the frustration, the mixture of hope and despair, into his novels.

Fielding's travelers "had no Objection to the Reasonableness of the Bill, but many to the Probability of paying it" (161; 2, 13): there is the basic problem of living in the modern world. Even if prices are not excessive, they may still be unaffordable. Adams, Joseph, and Fanny find themselves facing the same problem again and again, and their answer is never to bemoan their fate (which would be futile) but to ask for help. Fielding seems not to be offering us a commentary on the cost of living; that is neither his emphasis nor any part of his concern with the role of money in modern society. The pattern of events in the novel—those that have some connection with money, at any rate—suggests that Fielding uses money, as he uses other things, as a vehicle for contrasting generosity and parsimony, which become virtue and vice.

The travelers repeatedly find themselves in the same situations: they never have any money and are always in debt. Of itself it is not a particularly interesting situation, but it is a common one, and one that most of us would prefer not to be in unless we are unusually brazen. (Besides, we now have institutionalized consumer debt by way of the credit card, which removes some of the embarrassment.) At one of the inns, Joseph realizes that the "generous Gentleman" whose pleasure is to make promises he cannot keep, "instead of doing us any Service, hath left us the whole Reckoning to pay" (176–77; 2, 16). As readers, we no doubt wonder how they are going to get out of this one. They get out of it because they are honest:

> Adams . . . declared, "he had never read of such a Monster; but what vexes me most," says he, "is, that he hath decoyed us into running up a long Debt with you, which we are not able to pay; for we have no Money about us; and what is worse, live at such a distance, that if you should trust us, I am afraid you would lose your Money, for want of our finding any Conveniency of sending it." "Trust you, Master!" says the Host, "that I will with all my heart; I honour the Clergy too much to deny trusting one of them for such a Trifle; besides, I like your fear of never paying me. I have lost many a Debt in my Life-time; but was promised to be paid them all in a very short time. I will score this Reckoning for the Novelty of it. It is the first I do assure you of its kind." (177; 2, 16)

The scene proves a number of points: the host is a kind, hearty fellow—though that does not prevent him and Adams from having a furious argument over a free beer in the next chapter; people frequently abscond without paying their debts; no one has ever been this honest about a debt before. It is a part of the novel's thematic scheme that whenever Adams demonstrates his honesty, it comes across as naïveté. Adams is artless because he knows no other way, and so he could not be disingenuous even if he tried. He is therefore ignorant of the ways of the world: that is his innocence. And since innocence *is* ignorance (remember *Paradise Lost*), his honesty in a situation like this one at the inn is primal, utterly untainted by the material world. No wonder, then, that the innkeeper has never encountered honesty like his before.

In effect, Adams is establishing his credit by telling the host that he does not have any. A revolutionary (though I know of none writing in 1742) could use this conversational exchange to subvert the modern world of deficit financing, which enabled national trade and commerce to function on a network of credit and debt. A reformer perhaps but certainly no revolutionary, Fielding does not condemn the system, but he certainly deplores the materialism and greed of some of the system's managers and beneficiaries. He does not oppose financial capitalism, but he detests Peter Pounce, who is a typical representative of the new capitalism. In the earlier eighteenth century, people were talking for the first time about how much a man was worth, as if the value of a life could be measured in cash. A now obscure journalist named Charles Povey recorded this new way of seeing people: "A Man is not look'd upon for what Excellency is lodg'd in his Mind, but is valued according to the Wealth he enjoys: Instances of this kind are as common as the Rising of the Sun."[49] We should recognize the sign that Pounce is one of the new rich, one of the moneyed men who had risen to prominence and power since 1688. Adams tells him:

> "I have often heard you say it, that your Wealth is of your own Acquisition, and can it be credible that in your short time you should have amassed such a heap of Treasure as these People will have you worth? Indeed had you inherited an Estate like Sir *Thomas Booby*, which had descended in your Family for many Generations, they might have had a colour for their Assertions." "Why, what do they say I am worth?" cries *Peter* with a malicious Sneer. (275; 3, 13)

The answer, incongruously, is £20,000 though Adams thinks that so high a figure might offend Pounce, and so he says he believes it must be half that really. The truth is that Peter Pounce has amassed many times that amount, "and as to what you believe, or they believe, I care not a Fig, no not a Fart" (276; 3, 12). Pounce is therefore an offensive character in his own right, but it is really his attitude to money, rather than the fact that the system enables him to acquire it, that is in focus here. Adams, as usual, has not the slightest idea of the value of money, and does not realize that the rich are not flattered when you tell them you think they must be poor. In one of the novel's familiar formulations, Pounce comes off morally second best to Adams in a scene contrasting them. The scene ends with Adams leaping from the moving coach, and it begins with the two men defining charity: "Sir," said *Adams*, "my Definition of Charity is a generous Disposition to relieve the Distressed" (274; 3, 13). That is about as straightforward as you can get. But, typical of a lawyer, Pounce seizes on the word "disposition" and distinguishes it from the act: you can be disposed to give, but not actually do so, and that would still be charity. He then dismisses "the distressed" by saying "the Distresses of Mankind are mostly imaginary, and it would be rather Folly than Goodness to relieve them," and proceeds to complain about how much the law obliges him to pay to the poor out of his income from the land. (Not very much, in truth.)

Even if Pounce is representative of one who exploits the system of credit and financing that I call financial capitalism, the closest Fielding comes to condemning the system itself occurs in his description of Trulliber's surprise when Adams asks him for the small sum of seven shillings:

> Suppose a Stranger, who entered the Chambers of a Lawyer, being imagined a Client, when the Lawyer was preparing his Palm for the Fee, should pull out a Writ against him. Suppose an Apothecary, at the Door of a Chariot containing some great Doctor of eminent Skill, should, instead of Directions to a Patient, present him with a Potion for himself. Suppose a Minister should, instead of a good round Sum, treat my Lord— or Sir— or Esq;— with a good

Broomstick. Suppose a civil Companion, or a led Captain [a syco-phantic follower] should, instead of Virtue, and Honour, and Beauty, and Parts [wit], and Admiration, thunder Vice and Infamy, and Ugliness, and Folly, and Contempt, in his Patron's Ears. Sup-pose when a Tradesman first carries in his Bill, the Man of Fashion should pay it; or suppose, if he did so, the Tradesman should abate what he had overcharged, on the Supposition of waiting. In short—suppose what you will, you never can nor will suppose any thing equal to the Astonishment which seiz'd on *Trulliber*, as soon as *Adams* had ended his Speech. (165–66; 2, 14)

The narrative here combines money with flattery, the expected easy pickings of doctor and apothecary, the expected bribery by a minister (of state, that is) of people with fancy titles and high social status, the flattery expected of an underling, the assumption that high-class peo-ple never pay their bills on time and so tradesmen overcharge to com-pensate for the delays. Money is thus built into a sequence that reveals hypocrisy, cheating, and vanity. This was the way of the world, as countless examples would confirm.

We have met Fielding's "catalog" technique before—in which he piles up example after example as a satiric roster of infamous behav-ior. The technique is so blatant that it should remind readers of the earlier instance, the "Statue of Surprize" sequence, which reveals Lady Booby's astonishment when Joseph upholds his virtue. It should re-mind us of that, because it is surely meant to do so. Trulliber is just as immoral as Lady Booby, but the focus here is on money, not sex; on lack of charity, not lack of chastity. Trulliber is "reputed a Man of great Charity: for tho' he never gave a Farthing, he had always that Word in his Mouth" (169; 2, 15), in parallel to Lady Booby, one of those who, "tho' their Virtue remains unsullied, yet now and then some small Arrows will glance on the Shadow of it, their Reputation" (27; 1, 4). Lady Booby is not charitable either: she collects "all her Rents" while she is in London, but spends not a shilling on her tenants, "which tended not a little to their utter impoverishing," even though her family could keep the local population employed and fed with "scarce a visible Effect on their Benefactor's Pockets" (277; 4, 1). The structural suggestion of a parallel between Lady Booby and Parson Trulliber is significant because it shows that charity and chastity are not to be found where you might expect them. The rich can afford to be charitable, but they are not; the clergy of all people ought to be charitable, but they are not. Sexual fidelity can hardly be the province of rich or poor, but the architect John Gwynn, for instance, just assumed that the rich set an example that improved the morals of "useful and laborious people"—this in 1766.[50] At least Fielding's novel tells us that sexual infidelity, or unchastity, is to be found at the top of the social ladder, while fidelity is at the bottom. Sex and money therefore do belong together in the conceptual framework of the novel's morality. Whatever else we learn about money, we know that Adams, the good man, never has enough of it, and in the real modern world most people do not willingly part with it.

Two of the character types in Fielding's catalog of surprized people are a doctor and a lawyer, both of whom are represented elsewhere in the novel, and in no very flattering light. They are traditional targets of the satirist, and Fielding's satiric exposure of their greed is in fact fairly conventional. What is more, the "catalog" technique, though not new, was given a special kind of force because Swift used it so effectively in *Gulliver's Travels*, where the people he lists seem to have nothing in common until we realize that there is some covert evil linking them. Swift also acidly pointed out that "the rich Man enjoyed the Fruit of the poor Man's Labour, and the latter were a Thousand to One in Proportion to the former. That the Bulk of our People was forced to live miserably, by labouring every Day for small Wages to make a few live plentifully."[51] Swift did not specify sums of money, but Fielding, again giving his novel the flavor of being up to date, did. The sums of money Fielding's characters handle are nearly meaningless to us now, until we realize that Adams, who is obviously poor, is paid £23 a year, while Wilson can be sued for £3,000 damages, "which much distressed my Fortune to pay" (211; 3, 3), and can receive a £200 bank note—nearly nine times Adams's annual income. We know therefore that there is an enormous gulf between rich and poor, a gulf that charity would occasionally help to reduce. But the point is not that Fielding calls for a redistribution of wealth in society as Swift appears to do, nor is it that Fielding thinks the poor should live at the expense of the rich: it is that when the poor need help, which is not always, the rich should help. But they never do.

Adams, in fact, does not consider himself "very poor" and thinks that a half guinea would be "sufficient to bear our Expences in a noble manner" (248; 3, 7). He is of course wrong, because that amount of money would disappear in one or two nights at an inn.[52] At one such inn, Adams "declared he had eat his homely Commons, with much greater Satisfaction than his splendid Dinner, and exprest great Contempt for the Folly of Mankind, who sacrificed their Hopes of Heaven to the Acquisition of vast Wealth, since so much Comfort was to be found in the humblest State and the lowest Provision" (252; 3, 8). Adams's contempt for riches is all very well in theory, but it does not work in practice, as the novel reminds us every time a bill has to be paid. His perfectly admirable but impractical view is shared by the Catholic clergyman who asks him for charity, which to his great distress he cannot give because his half guinea has been stolen. Says the clergyman, "I have often been as much surprized as you are, when I consider the Value which Mankind in general set on Riches, since every day's Experience shews us how little is in their power" (252; 3, 8). The two men then go on to amplify that attitude with numerous examples of what money cannot buy.

Fielding's emphasis throughout *Joseph Andrews* is on the moral and immoral qualities of people in Britain in his time. One major factor that influences morality is money. Fielding does not call for an overhaul of financial capitalism, yet he recognizes that it places so much value on money that it produces social imbalance, venality, parsimony, luxury, and misery:

In fact, when I consider any social system that prevails in the modern world, I can't, so help me God, see it as anything but a conspiracy of the rich to advance their own interests under the pretext of organizing society. They think up all sorts of tricks and dodges, first for keeping safe their ill-gotten gains, and then for exploiting the poor by buying their labour as cheaply as possible. Once the rich have decided that these tricks and dodges shall be officially recognized by society—which includes the poor as well as the rich—they acquire the force of law.

These are not Fielding's words, however: they are spoken by Raphael, at the end of one of the greatest of all satires, *Utopia*.[53]

Appendix: British Money

Today British currency is based on the decimal system, with 100 pence equal to a pound (also called the pound sterling). Decimal currency was adopted in 1971, when the old coins were given new values and subsequently withdrawn from circulation. Before 1971, currency used to be a far more complicated and confusing affair, which always appeared to Britain's foreign visitors to be part of a xenophobic conspiracy.

Bills (known in Britain as notes or bank notes) now come from the Bank of England (and the Bank of Scotland), which was founded in 1694. But until 1833, when the Bank of England started issuing printed bills, people did not make ordinary purchases with printed money. There were bank notes, but they were hand written and had terminal dates on them; they were like negotiable checks. Most people used cash for everyday purposes.

The smallest unit of currency was the farthing, which was also physically a tiny coin. Two farthings made a halfpenny (pronounced hay-p'ny), two halfpennies made a penny. A penny bought a sixteen-ounce loaf of bread when Fielding wrote *Joseph Andrews*. Many consumer items were priced in fractions of a penny. There were objects that could be bought for a farthing, a halfpenny, three farthings, a penny-farthing (which in the nineteenth century became the name of a bicycle with a huge front wheel and a tiny rear wheel because the disparate sizes of the wheels looked like the coins), and a penny-halfpenny (also called three halfpence, pronounced three hay-p'nce). If you are talking of the physical coins, the plural of penny is pennies, but if you are talking about the value, the plural is pence (though you would never know it if you listened to Britons today who often refer to one pence), and so you might have two or three pennies in your hand, but the goods you want to buy would cost twopence (spelled as one word and pronounced tuppance) and threepence (pronounced thrupp'nce or threpp'nce). Pence, or pennies, are virtually worthless today, but when incomes and prices were lower, these humble coins had proportionally greater value.

As the American cent is designated by "¢," one might expect the penny to be "p." It is today, but today's pence are, formally and strictly speaking, called "new pence." In the old currency, the notation for a penny was "d." This is because British coins were designated (but not named) after coins that were used two thousand years earlier in imperial Rome. The Romans had a small coin called a denarius (pl. denarii), and the British used "d" (for denarius) for the formal designation of a penny. So "4d." meant fourpence (pronounced FOR-p'nce). In Fielding's day, coins were minted in denominations of a farthing, a halfpenny, and a penny, and some foreign coins also were in general circulation, with accepted British values. To make it all the more confusing, some values were expressed by using medieval and Tudor denominations, such as the groat and the mark. Farthings, halfpennies, and pennies were made from copper, and were sometimes called coppers.

Twelvepence constituted the next unit of currency, the shilling, also a denomination in the coinage, but this one contained silver. A shilling would buy a sixty-four-page pamphlet—roughly speaking, the equivalent of a paperback book today. Parson Adams tells Joseph Andrews to use all his money: "nine Shillings and three-pence-halfpenny" (67, 1, 15); on a price tag this would be written as 9s 3½d or sometimes just 9/3½. The shilling was therefore designated as "s." No, not "s" for shilling, but "s" for solidus (pl. solidi), another Latin coin.

Five shillings made a crown (there was such a coin), and two shillings and sixpence (called two and six) made a half crown (later minted as another coin). Twenty shillings made a pound. The symbol for a pound, £, refers to yet another Latin word, libra (pl. librae), which is the origin of today's Italian currency, the lira (pl. lire). Like the $ sign, the £ sign goes before the number, but sometimes, especially in eighteenth-century texts, it would be printed as a simple "l" or "*l*" and placed after the number: so five pounds might be printed as 5 *l.* The pound was actually an imaginary unit of currency (such imaginary units were also called moneys of account) in the eighteenth century, because there was no pound coin. Pound coins began to be minted in the nineteenth century, when they were also known as sovereigns.

Many prices were expressed in guineas (yet another coin, this one minted from gold and designated for once by English, not Latin: "gn" and "gns"). A guinea was usually worth twenty-one shillings, that is, one pound and one shilling (£ l, ls, or lgn). Two guineas would be two pounds two shillings (£2, 2s, or 2gns) and so on. Even though decimal currency made the shilling obsolete, and therefore also the guinea, one or two of London's most exclusive stores still hang on to the guinea as a unit for extremely expensive merchandise, but it involves ludicrous mathematical computation.

Parson Adams thinks his nine volumes of sermons are worth £100. If Adams had been famous, like Stephen King or Judith Krantz in the United States today, his name alone would have commanded such a price, but nobody was paid very much for sermons. Novelists sometimes fared a little better. Fielding's own recompense for writing *Joseph Andrews* was £183 and five shillings (£183 5s), and for *Tom Jones* he received the sizable sum of £600. But back in the 1660s, Milton was paid only £10 for *Paradise Lost,* or a farthing per line for the greatest poem in the language. Expecting £100, Parson Adams is as usual out of touch with reality.

Adams's annual income is only £23, about the same as a small farmer might earn. Only unskilled laborers, fishermen, and common soldiers and sailors were paid less. An average lawyer could expect to make £100 a year, but one notorious lawyer made much more. This financial wizard, who was also a genius at cheating his clients and manipulating the law, was Peter Walter, on whom Fielding modeled Peter Pounce. When Walter died in 1746, his estate was worth the staggering sum of £282,000. A university professor (always under-paid) made about £60 a year, shopkeepers any amount between £40 and £400. The very richest families enjoyed incomes of £20,000 a year, which (without even making adjustments for inflation) is a fairly good income in Britain today. Five incomes of £20,000 would make not a hundred grand but a "plum."

It is always difficult to estimate equivalents for these sums of money today. Price inflation in eighteenth-century Britain was slower and smaller (about 20 percent in all in one hundred years), and real wages went down. It is more sensible to think not of cash equivalents, but of equivalent purchasing power and consumer costs as a propor-tion of income. Peter Walter's estate was a fortune by any standards, but it was by no means the largest. The Duke of Chandos, who died in 1719, was a millionaire, an exceptionally rare species. At the other end of the economic scale, one family of farm laborers (about 1780) lived in an appalling one-room house for which they were being charged one shilling a week for rent; this was probably one-sixth of their poor income. As for consumer goods, a copy of *Joseph Andrews* itself cost 6s (six shillings), so for anyone earning less than about £40 a year, books were something of a luxury. Even Swift and Fielding, who needed books, possessed only about 500 titles by the time they died. The actual sum of money that Adams has, 9s 3½d, would have bought him two of the cheaper tickets at a theater in London, but to Adams that sum is a week's income.

Finally, as everyone knows, Benjamin Franklin said that the only two certainties in human life are death and taxes. Whatever the tax levels are, people always think they are too high, and the characters in *Joseph Andrews* are no exception. In eighteenth-century Britain there were taxes on commodities such as salt, soap, leather, wine, beer; on land; and on windows (which of course encouraged people to board up their windows and live unhealthily in the dark). But there was no tax on income. Those were the days.

Notes and References

1. F.T. Blanchard, *Fielding the Novelist: A Study in Historical Criticism* (New Haven: Yale University Press, 1926), 555.

2. Ibid., 562.

3. Ibid., 553. But *Amelia* was not the commercial disaster that Blanchard thought. See Martin C. Battestin's excellent introduction to the Wesleyan edition of *Amelia* (Oxford: Clarendon Press, 1983).

4. Recorded in a letter from Joseph to Thomas Warton, 29 October 1746, printed in John Wooll, *Biographical Memoirs of the Late Revd Joseph Warton, D. D.* (London, 1806), 215, which is in turn quoted by Blanchard, 13.

5. Simon Varey, *Henry Fielding* (Cambridge: Cambridge University Press, 1986), 60–61.

6. *Henry Fielding: The Critical Heritage,* ed. Ronald Paulson and Thomas Lockwood (London: Routledge & Kegan Paul, 1969), 121.

7. Ibid., 122.

8. Ibid., 118.

9. Ibid., 123.

10. Ibid., 128–129.

11. Battestin, introduction to *Joseph Andrews*, xxxiv–xxxv.

12. Murphy published his essay as an introduction to his edition of *The Works of Henry Fielding*, 4 vols. (London: A. Millar, 1762). Most of Murphy's essay is reprinted in *Critical Heritage*, 404–32. This quotation is from p. 423.

13. *Critical Heritage*, 421.

14. Ibid., 423.

15. Ibid., 159.

16. Ibid., 263.

17. Blanchard, *Fielding the Novelist*, 550.

18. Samuel Richardson, *Correspondence*, ed. Anna Laetitia Barbauld, vol. 4 (London: Richard Phillips, 1804), 60–61.

19. Wilbur L. Cross, *The History of Henry Fielding*, 3 vols. (New Haven: Yale University Press, 1918); James A. Work, "Henry Fielding, Christian Censor," in *The Age of Johnson: Essays Presented to Chauncy Brewster Tinker*, ed. Frederick W. Hilles (New Haven: Yale University Press, 1949), 139–48.

20. Martin C. Battestin, *The Moral Basis of Fielding's Art: A Study of Joseph Andrews* (Middletown, Conn.: Wesleyan University Press, 1959).

21. Arthur Sherbo, *Studies in the Eighteenth-Century English Novel* (East Lansing: Michigan State University Press, 1963), 104–19.

22. Ronald Paulson, *Fielding: A Collection of Critical Essays*, Twentieth Century Views (Englewood Cliffs, N.J.: Prentice-Hall, 1962), 2.

23. Preface to *Joseph Andrews*, Wesleyan Edition, 11.

24. For the idea of comedy as a celebration of a benign cosmic system, see also Battestin's much maligned study, *The Providence of Wit: Aspects of Form in Augustan Literature and the Arts* (Oxford: Clarendon Press, 1974), esp. 141.

25. Of all the published criticism on Fielding, 82 percent has been written by men, none of them so far receptive to feminism; the advisory board for the standard edition of Fielding's works consists of thirteen distinguished and experienced male scholars: eight of them are dead, four have retired, and the two youngest are over seventy.

26. Historians and political scientists sometimes complain that it is anachronistic to refer to the bourgeoisie in eighteenth-century Britain. Yet Fielding himself referred to merchants as "the bourgeois" in 1747.

27. P. K. Elkin, *The Augustan Defence of Satire* (Oxford: Clarendon Press, 1973), is useful in clarifying the distinction.

28. Preface to *Absalom and Achitophel* (1682) in *The Works of John Dryden*, vol. 2, ed. H. T. Swedenberg and Vinton Dearing (Berkeley and Los Angeles: University of California Press, 1972), 5.

29. Preface to *The Battel of the Books* (1710), in *Prose Works of Jonathan Swift*, vol. 1, ed. Herbert Davis (Oxford: Blackwell, 1957), 140.

30. *Gulliver's Travels*, in *Prose Works of Jonathan Swift*, vol. 11, ed. Herbert Davis, rev. ed. (Oxford: Blackwell, 1959), 250.

31. Ibid., 248.

32. *Clarissa*, ed. Angus Ross (New York: Viking, 1985), 1213.

33. C. J. Rawson, *Henry Fielding and the Augustan Ideal Under Stress* (London: Routledge & Kegan Paul, 1972), 5.

34. The best discussion of mock-epic is Geoffrey Tillotson's introduction to Pope's *Rape of the Lock and Other Poems*, Twickenham Edition, 3d

ed. (London: Methuen; New Haven: Yale University Press, 1962), 106–12.

35. Fielding styled himself H. Scriblerus Secundus, that is H[enry] Scribbler the Second, in 1730.

36. William Freedman, "*Joseph Andrews:* Clothing and the Concretization of Character," *Discourse* 4 (1961): 304–10, discusses only Adams.

37. Barthes, *The Pleasure of the Text,* trans. Richard Miller (New York: Hill & Wang, 1975).

38. See my discussion in *Henry Fielding,* 46–51.

39. David Foxon, *Libertine Literature in England 1660–1745* ([London], 1964), reprinted from *The Book Collector* 12 (1963), 21–36, 159–77, 294–307, 476–87.

40. Fielding, *Miscellanies,* vol. 1, ed. Henry Knight Miller ([Middletown, Conn.:] Wesleyan University Press, 1972), preface, 4.

41. *Complete Works of Henry Fielding,* ed. W. E. Henley, vol. 13 (1903; New York: Barnes & Noble, 1967), 19.

42. James A. Work, "Henry Fielding: Christian Censor," in *The Age of Johnson,* 139–48.

43. The sale catalog of Fielding's library is reprinted in Ethel M. Thornbury, *Henry Fielding's Theory of the Comic Prose Epic* (1931; New York: Russell & Russell, 1966), 168–89.

44. *Moral Basis,* 150.

45. For succinct, pertinent commentary on the pastoral, see Maynard Mack, *Alexander Pope: A Life* (New York: Norton, 1985), 134–40.

46. Swift, *Prose Works,* 11: 196.

47. *Moral Basis,* 32.

48. Cf. ibid., 44–51.

49. Charles Povey, *Visions of Sir Heister Ryley,* no. 61, 8 January 1711.

50. John Gwynn, *London and Westminster Improved* (London: for the author, 1766), viii.

51. Swift, *Prose Works,* 11: 251.

52. The bill at the inn is seven shillings. Half as much again would make exactly half a guinea.

53. Thomas More, *Utopia,* trans. Paul Turner (Harmondsworth, England: Penguin, 1965), 130.

Glossary

The following words and phrases, all of which occur in *Joseph Andrews,* were in common use in Fielding's day. Some of them have fallen into disuse now, and some have changed their meanings, and so tend to mislead us.

admire (43; 1, 9)   wonder at; be surprised by; the word did not yet mean "hold in high esteem."

banns (282; 4, 2)   a proclamation by a clergyman, announcing an intended marriage between two people, one of whom would normally be resident in his parish. The practice of "publishing the banns" is still in use in the Church of England.

beau (194; 3, 2)   (plural: beaus, or more correctly, beaux) a dandy or elegantly dressed gentleman; "a man of dress; a man whose great care is to deck [ornament] his person" (Johnson's *Dictionary*).

caale vurst (165; 2, 14)   call first; the peculiar spelling is meant to denote Parson Trulliber's pronunciation with a heavy local accent.

cap (146; 2, 11)	in the expression "to cap verses," to quote a line of verse whose first word begins with a particular letter, such as the last letter of the last word of the previously quoted line. Capping verses was a game played by two or more people using verbal dexterity and their memory for poetry. The precise rules varied a great deal.
chair (9; preface)	a sedan chair, that is, a chair enclosed rather like a cabin, lifted and carried on poles by two men known as chairmen.
chopping (337; 4, 15)	a slang term, used only of children: sturdy, healthy, thriving.
closet (33; 1, 6)	a small, private room (not a cupboard or storage area).
clout (332; 4, 14)	cloth, or shift. Slipslop's double clout is (presumably) a cloth folded double.
coach and six (74; 1, 16)	a coach drawn by six horses. These were expensive to buy and maintain, and so were something of a status symbol.
crabstick (137; 2, 9)	a stick cut from a branch of a crab apple, or crab tree.
cure (281; 4, 2)	curacy; the office of a curate, or parish priest.
curtains (330; 4, 14)	curtains that are hung around a four-poster bed, not across a window.
didapper (312; 4, 9)	an alternative name for the dabchick, or small grebe. Thus Beau Didapper is named for a bird.
discovering (343; 4, 16)	dis-covering, or taking a cover off.

eat (326; 4, 13)	past tense of the verb "to eat," probably pronounced "et"; the same as the word now spelled "ate."
Falmouth (179; 2, 17)	a small fishing port in Cornwall, in the southwestern corner of England.
footman	"a low menial servant in livery," according to Johnson's *Dictionary*. A footman's job was to attend his employer at table, to open doors, to help the employer and guests in and out of carriages, and so on. Because footmen and valets walked behind their employers in public, they were vulgarly called "fart catchers" (Grose's *Dictionary of Slang*).
French distemper (179; 2, 17)	syphilis.
goal (179; 2, 17)	jail, and apparently pronounced like "jail," too. The modern British spelling is "gaol."
hagged out (333; 4, 14)	used here to mean tired out, fatigued; it usually meant harassed. In modern British usage it has been replaced by "fagged out" or even "shagged out" to mean exhausted.
Ifaukins (298; 4, 6)	an almost meaningless exclamation, carrying a vaguely scornful overtone.
instances (340; 4, 16)	urgent, pressing requests.
lopped (290; 4, 5)	allowed to hang down.
make love (324; 4, 12)	express affection (with no connotation of having sexual intercourse). Men and women might make love to each other when they were a thousand miles apart, by writing flirtatious letters.

Glossary

naked (332; 4, 14) bare (as now), but the culture of the time considered someone to be naked even if he was not completely bare. A man in his underwear, like Parson Adams in the confused bedroom scenes, would be considered naked.

parts (165; 2, 14) abilities; qualities; powers, usually of the mind.

penknife (193; 3, 2) pocket knife. (The word survives in modern British usage.) So called because it was originally used to cut and sharpen pens, when they were made from quills.

pepper (74; 1, 16) used punningly here; "to pepper" is to spray with bullets, but it also means to infect someone with venereal disease.

quality (296; 4, 6) upper class, when used in expressions like "a person of quality."

small beer (307; 4, 8) dilute beer, or weak beer. Not some kind of cheat, just a mild drink. In the twentieth century, something very similar to this type of beer came to be known as "mild" and can still occasionally be found.

smoaking (146; 2, 11) alternative spelling of "smoking"; finding out, penetrating a disguise.

sneaking (190; 3, 1) servile, mean, low (rather than furtive or cowardly).

vailes (176; 2, 16) money given to servants; tips.

Selected Bibliography

Primary Works

Joseph Andrews, ed. Martin C. Battestin. Middletown, Conn.: Wesleyan University Press, 1967. The Wesleyan Edition of Fielding's works has so far also published *Miscellanies*, vol. 1 (1972); *Tom Jones*, 2 vols. (1974); *The Jacobite's Journal* (1974); *Amelia* (1983); *The True Patriot and Related Writings* (1987); *The Covent-Garden Journal* (1988); and *An Enquiry into the Causes of the Late Increase of Robbers* (1988).

Joseph Andrews and Shamela, ed. Martin C. Battestin. Riverside Edition. Boston: Houghton Mifflin, 1961.

Joseph Andrews and Shamela, ed. Martin C. Battestin with introduction and notes by Douglas Brooks-Davies. World's Classics. Oxford: Oxford University Press, 1980.

The Complete Works of Henry Fielding, ed. W. E. Henley. 16 vols. 1903; New York: Barnes & Noble, 1967.

Secondary Works

Books

Alter, Robert. *Fielding and the Nature of the Novel.* Cambridge, Mass.: Harvard University Press, 1968. Good, useful introduction.

Battestin, Martin C. *The Moral Basis of Fielding's Art: A Study of "Joseph Andrews"* (Middletown, Conn.: Wesleyan University Press, 1959). Essential background for a reading of this novel's moral concerns.

Blanchard, Frederic T. *Fielding the Novelist: A Study in Historical Criticism.*

New Haven: Yale University Press, 1926. A survey of the critical reception of the novels.

Cross, Wilbur L. *The History of Henry Fielding*. 3 vols. New Haven: Yale University Press, 1918. The standard biography, now superseded by Martin C. and Ruthe R. Battestin's *Henry Fielding: A Life* (London & New York: Routledge, 1989).

Goldberg, Homer. *The Art of "Joseph Andrews"*. Chicago: University of Chicago Press, 1969. A study of Fielding's sources: Cervantes, Lesage, Marivaux, and Scarron. The emphasis is thus on romance.

Johnson, Maurice. *Fielding's Art of Fiction*. Philadelphia: University of Pennsylvania Press, 1961. A collection of barely related essays. The one on *Joseph Andrews* (47–60) claims that it starts as burlesque and finishes as romance.

Paulson, Ronald, and Lockwood, Thomas, eds. *Henry Fielding: The Critical Heritage*. London: Routledge & Kegan Paul, 1969. Indispensable for the early record of reactions to Fielding's works.

Rogers, Pat. *Henry Fielding*. New York: Scribner's, 1983. A concise, attractively written biography.

Varey, Simon. *Henry Fielding*. Cambridge: Cambridge University Press, 1986. An introduction to the major works.

Wright, Andrew. *Henry Fielding: Mask and Feast*. Berkeley: University of California Press, 1965. On the festive comedy of the novels. Good on *Joseph Andrews* and *Tom Jones*, but not on *Amelia*, which is not festive and does not fit the book's scheme.

Articles

Battestin, Martin C. "Fielding's Changing Politics and *Joseph Andrews*." *Philological Quarterly* 39 (1960): 39–55. On Fielding's relations with Walpole and his attitude to politics in 1740–41. Circumstantial evidence, but useful all the same.

Battestin, Martin C. "Lord Hervey's Role in *Joseph Andrews*." *Philological Quarterly* 42 (1963): 226–41. Lord Hervey was the model for Beau Didapper.

Cauthen, I. B., Jr. "Fielding's Digressions in *Joseph Andrews*." *College English* 17 (1956): 379–82. Argues that the interpolated stories are variations on the novel's moral and aesthetic themes.

Ehrenpreis, Irvin. "Fielding's Use of Fiction: The Autonomy of *Joseph Andrews*." In *Twelve Original Essays on Great English Novels*, edited by C. Shapiro, 23–41. Detroit: Wayne State University Press, 1960. An important essay that argues convincingly for the unity of *Joseph Andrews*.

Goldberg, Homer. "The Interpolated Stories in *Joseph Andrews* or 'The History of the World in General' Satirically Revised." *Modern Philology* 63 (1966): 295–310. Possibly overdoing it, Goldberg explores Fielding's debt to Cervantes and his parody (so it is claimed) of *Don Quixote* at key moments.

Reid, B. L. "Utmost Merriment, Strictest Decency: *Joseph Andrews*." *Sewanee Review* 75 (1967): 559–84. Connects goodwill (a major theme, Reid says) with various incidents in the plot.

Spilka, Mark. "Comic Resolution in Fielding's *Joseph Andrews*." *College English* 15 (1953): 11–19. Spilka finds more than just uproarious comedy in the bedroom scenes, but he reads perhaps too much seriousness into the mistakes of the night.

Weinbrot, Howard. "Chastity and Interpolation: Two Aspects of *Joseph Andrews*." *Journal of English and Germanic Philology* 69 (1970): 14–31. Joseph's chastity is normative, not laughable, Weinbrot argues. And the interpolated stories contrast the comic world with violence and misery.

Bibliography

Cross, Wilbur L. *The History of Henry Fielding.* Vol. 3. New Haven: Yale University Press, 1918.

Hahn, H. George. *Henry Fielding: An Annotated Bibliography.* Metuchen, N. J., and London: Scarecrow Press, 1979. Lists all of Fielding's works and all the major criticism published up to the mid-1970s. Each entry is sensibly annotated. Some of Hahn's comments are themselves penetrating criticism and should be consulted.

Index

Index

war, 80
Wesley, John, 96
Whitefield, George, 96

Wild, Jonathan, 79
William III, 3
Work, James A., 17, 88

The Author

A Londoner who now lives in Los Angeles, Simon Varey was educated at Cambridge University and taught English literature for nine years at the University of Utrecht before leaving the Netherlands for the more hospitable climate of Southern California. He has edited a collection of Lord Bolingbroke's political essays, *Contributions to the "Craftsman"* (1982), and written a book on Bolingbroke (1984), and another on Fielding (1986). His ambitious study, *Space and the Eighteenth-Century English Novel,* has been recently published by Cambridge University Press. He is now working with Howard Erskine-Hill on an anthology of Jacobite poetry, and is editing two seventeenth- and eighteenth-century cookery manuscripts and Lord Bolingbroke's correspondence. Varey is a gourmet cook and casual food historian who has earned his living until recently by teaching English at the University of California, Los Angeles.